MIDLOTHIAN PUBLIC LIBRARY

3 1614 00107 9400

 **W9-AOR-809**

MIDLOTHIAN PUBLIC LIBRARY

thAt's

mAgic!

Midlothian
Public Library

14701 S. Kenton Ave.
Midlothian, IL 60445

BAKER & TAYLOR

thAt's mAgic!

RichARd jones

NEW HOLLAND

MIDLOTHIAN PUBLIC LIBRARY
14701 S. KENTON AVE.
MIDLOTHIAN, IL 60445

This edition published in 2003 by **New Holland Publishers (UK) Ltd**

London • Cape Town • Sydney • Auckland

2 4 6 8 10 9 7 5 3

Garfield House, 86-88 Edgware Road, London W2 2EA, United Kingdom

www.newhollandpublishers.com

80 McKenzie Street, Cape Town 8001, South Africa

Level 1/Unit 4, 14 Aquatic Drive, Frenchs Forest, NSW 2086, Australia

218 Lake Road, Northcote, Auckland, New Zealand

First published in 2001

Copyright © 2001 in text Richard Jones

Copyright © 2001 in photographs Sean East

Copyright © 2001 New Holland Publishers (UK) Ltd

All rights reserved. No part of this publication may be reproduced, stored in a retrieval
system or transmitted, in any form or by any means, electronic, mechanical,
photocopying, recording or otherwise, without the prior written permission of the
publishers and copyright holders.

ISBN 1 85974 935 6

Publishing Manager: **Jo Hemmings**
Editor: **Michaella Standen**
Copy Editor: **Jill Harvey**
Design and Cover Design: **Balley Design Associates**
Index: **Sandra Shotter**
Production: **Joan Woodroffe**

Reproduction by Modern Age Repro Co. Ltd., Hong Kong
Printed and bound in Malaysia by Times Offset (M) Sdn Bhd

'The *most beautiful experience* we can have *is* the *mysterious*. It *is* the FUNDAMENtAl emotion which stands At the cRAdle OF true ARt ANd true science. Whoever does not know it And can no longer wonder, no longer mARvel, *is* As good As deAd, ANd h*is* eyes ARe dimmed.'

albert einstein.

The pursuit of magic is both fascinating and entertaining. Its exponents, whether amateur hobbyists or top professionals, are part of a worldwide community that can communicate through a shared interest, irrespective of cultural or language barriers.

In the pages that follow, you will find an introduction to the world of magic through learning to perform over forty magical routines. None require investment in expensive apparatus – a few decks of cards, a length of rope and the occasional envelope are all you will need in your bag of tricks. Most can be done at a moment's notice, and many can even be done with borrowed props.

It is my sincere hope that this book will encourage you to develop an interest in magic. You may choose to remain a hobbyist – some of magic's greatest inventors have been those who indulge in it as a hobby. You may choose to take it further, study in depth, or take it up as a profession. Whichever you do, magic offers many and varied opportunities to meet new and exciting people, whether at international conventions or at a local level through clubs and societies.

Enjoy!

Richard Jones

8 ★ that's magic!

MAGiCA1

MAGiCA1 HistORY

a jouRNey throUgh time For us, living in the 21st century, awe and wonderment have been largely eroded by the advances of science. But our distant ancestors inhabited a fearsome and hostile world. As they struggled to understand the swings of nature, these primitive peoples were only too willing to respect and reward anyone they believed capable of understanding and controlling this dangerous environment. Thus were born the earliest practitioners of magic.

As the millennia rolled by, these wonder-workers evolved into the fakirs, witch doctors and shamans of early civilizations. They laid the foundations for the priests and soothsayers of Egypt, Greece and Rome, with their magnificent temples in which awe-struck mortals could witness spectacular illusions: altar fires that would explode into jets of searing, bright flame; doors that would be opened by invisible hands, and horns and trumpets that played of their own accord. These elaborate illusions helped create the atmosphere in which the gods could utter their commandments, and oracles could reveal what the fates had in store.

Meanwhile, on the streets of these great empires, the forebears of our modern magicians were busily astounding their audiences. These entertainers wandered from town to town exhibiting their skills wherever they could find an audience, and gravitating towards the great public games and religious festivals. The more accomplished would find themselves appearing in the established theatres, or would

MAGICAL

MAGICAL MAGICAL

be booked to amuse guests at great banquets. Many, no doubt, followed the Roman legions as they swept across Western Europe and found their way into Britain. As the Roman Empire collapsed, historical records became sparse, and it would be another four hundred years before Europe emerged from the so-called 'Dark Ages'.

From the 8th century onwards, itinerant entertainers swarmed across Europe. Several achieved considerable respectability; they were called upon to entertain royalty and nobility, and were suitably rewarded. Others found their talents in demand for more inspirational services. Just before the Battle of Hastings in 1066, for example, we learn how Taillifer appeared before the Norman soldiers and performed 'many marvellous feats of dexterity, throwing up and catching his lance and sword, so that they all considered him an enchanter or conjuror'.

By the 1100s, sleight-of-hand performers had become known as jugglers, who found themselves being constantly censured by officialdom. In 1106 they were forbidden to reside in certain French cities. In 1150, St Bernard of Clairvaux preached that 'the tricks of jugglers never please God', and a hundred years later, Louis IX vowed to drive them out of France.

Despite this persecution they persevered, and several contemporary accounts of their activities have survived. We learn of a Dutch juggler who in 1272 cut off a boy's head, then restored his victim to life. A performer was even said to have thrown his pony's bridle into the air, whereupon he, his wife, their maid and the pony all climbed

MAGICAL HISTORY

up it and vanished from mortal view. It is somewhat anticlimactic to learn that they were subsequently discovered drunk in a nearby tavern!

Meanwhile, the Crusades had opened up the vast and mystical knowledge of the Arab world, in particular Moorish scientists' investigations into the secret art of the ancient Egyptian goldsmiths. The Arabs called Egypt Khem and the art of working with gold *al-kimiya*, 'the art of the land of Khem'. Whether or not this was the origin of the word alchemy is debatable but, with the Moorish occupation of Spain, their knowledge found its way into Europe and inspired the legendary search for the Philosopher's Stone.

The magicians and alchemists, many of them clerics, strove to turn base metals into gold, among other things; their research therefore laid the foundations of modern chemistry, mathematics and science. But they also created numerous ingenious illusions, many of which would later be rediscovered and adapted by stage illusionists.

Whereas the Christian church was willing to countenance the studies and illusions of its own clerics to an extent, it was equally willing to attribute similar feats to demonic assistance when done by the laity. Fuelled by the paranoia of fanatical clerics, who came to see the devil's hand in any number of innocent pastimes, the infamous witch-hunts began. Over a period of two hundred years close on 40,000 unfortunate souls, some of whom were, doubtless, no more than sleight-of-hand performers, were executed as witches.

It was against this backcloth of zealous fanaticism that in 1581, Margaret Simons

AgiCAl
MAGiCAl MAGiCAl

appeared before Justice of the Peace Reginald Scott, charged with witchcraft. Stunned by the pointless cruelty of the persecution, Scott devoted the next three years to constructing a well-researched argument that, he hoped, would explode the ludicrous superstitions. In 1584 he published *The Discoverie Of Witchcraft*, which showed

how jugglers and popular entertainers, using natural rather than supernatural means, could easily reproduce the marvels supposedly performed by witches.

The section entitled 'The Art of Juggling Discovered' revealed, for the first time in print, the secrets behind the tricks performed by the juggling fraternity. The book caused a sensation and was later denounced by King James I, who had all obtainable copies seized and burnt by the public executioner.

Scott inspired many imitators. Books on how to do magic became the vogue in the 17th and 18th centuries, as it came to be seen as nothing more than harmless entertainment. Chief among these were the Hocus Pocus books, first published in 1635, which appeared in various editions for the next two hundred years.

As the superstitions of the past gave way to the 'Age of Reason', magicians began to perform at indoor venues where the audience would come to them, rather than vice versa. Able to charge admission and freed from the need to carry their props from town to town, they were able to develop more complex and spectacular illusions.

The most famous of this new breed of magician was Isaac Fawkes (also spelt Fawks

MAGiCA1 HiStORY

and Faux) who was immortalised by artist William Hogarth in his engraving *Southwark Fair* (1733). Nobleman and commoner alike attended Fawkes's performances and, such was his success that, by the time of his death in 1733 he had amassed a considerable fortune of around £10,000.

The use of animals also became fashionable. 'Learned' pigs, dogs, horses and cats, able to identify chosen cards and read spectators' minds, proved extremely popular. Capelli, an Italian conjuror, even had a company of cats, whose talents included the ability to play the organ, hammer upon an anvil and one cat that could understand both French and Italian! Dr Samuel Johnson commented wryly on one porcine performer that

'Had he been illiterate he had long since been smoked into hams... Now he is visited by the philosopher and the politician... and gratified with the murmur of applause...'

With the dawn of the 19th century, several magicians began to capitalize on their occult roots by astounding, astonishing and outright terrifying their audiences with illusions that seemed to summon spirits of the dead and fiery demons before their very eyes. These 'Ghost Shows', despite eclipsing the popularity of sleight of hand for a time, gave mystery and spectacle to the magicians' art; the origins of many modern stage illusions can be traced back to these 'Phantasmagoria'.

One of the most influential magicians of the age was John Henry Anderson the self-proclaimed 'Wizard of the North' who, realising the importance of hype never missed

AgiCA1
MAgiCA1 MAgiCA1

an advertising opportunity. His spectacular stage shows were announced with gaudy and boastful posters, plastered across such imaginative locations as the cliffs at Niagara Falls or even the sides of the pyramids in Egypt! His street parades set a trend that was eagerly followed by circuses, and his charitable performances raised so much money that he was made a life governor of eight British Hospitals.

It is the French magician Robert Houdin who is acclaimed as the father of modern conjuring. Born Jean Eugene Robert in 1805, he performed fairground escapes in his youth before settling down to the watchmakers' trade. Then, at the age of forty, he decided to become a professional conjuror. He combined his surname with his wife's maiden name and Robert Houdin's magical career began. Whereas until then stage magicians had appeared in long flowing robes, he appeared in a simple tail coat. Audiences marvelled at his sensational illusions, such as an orange tree that blossomed and bore fruit while being circled by mechanical butterflies. The incredible levitation of his young son became legendary. His secrets have inspired generations of magicians and still continue to do so.

A final influential figure of the late 19th century was Angelo Lewis who, in 1875, published the world's first noteworthy magical textbook. Using the pen name 'Professor Hoffman' his was the first publication to instruct readers the all-important *how* to perform magic rather than to simply detail how tricks were done.

As the 19th turned into the 20th century Chinese Magicians came into vogue. Ching

MAGICA1
MAGiCA1 HistORY

Ling Foo (1854–1918), a favourite of the Empress of China, arrived in America in the 1890s where his novel and exotic style caused a sensation. In 1899 he pledged $1000 to anyone who could exactly duplicate his act. The challenge was accepted by 'resting' magician William Ellsworth Robinson (1861–1918) who was turned away because he wasn't Chinese and could not, therefore, duplicate the act exactly. Enraged by this obvious dupe, Robinson retaliated by assuming a Chinese identity, called himself Chung Ling Soo and eclipsed Foo in both fame and fortune. He died on 23rd March 1918 when a faulty mechanism, caused his famous bullet catching routine to go tragically wrong, before a live audience at the Empire Theatre, Wood Green, London. Only then did many people realise that he was American rather than Chinese!

Magicians at large, however, had discovered the music halls and variety theatres. John Neville Maskelyne and David Devant were astounding their audiences with breathtaking illusions, while the likes of Fred Culpitt and American Frank Von Hoven recognized the importance of laughter and created comedy acts – the latter drawing laughter from the fact that his tricks always went wrong.

The most famous 20th-century magician, perhaps even of all time, was born Ehric Weiss in Appleton, Wisconsin on 6 April 1874. Having discovered a battered copy of *The Memoirs of Robert Houdin* in a second-hand bookstore, he was inspired to take up magic, added an 'i' to his idol's name (giving it the literal meaning 'like Houdin') and became Harry Houdini. His daring and sensational escapes, coupled with his

AGiCA1
MAGiCA1 MAGiCA1

substantial talent for self-publicity, brought him international fame and considerable fortune. Since his death from peritonitis on Halloween 1926 he has achieved legendary if not mythical status, and his name is known the world over.

With the advent of cinema, magicians and illusionists had to work ever harder at presenting grand illusions. The likes of Howard Thurston and Harry Jansen (known to his audiences as Dante) staged spectacular shows, the latter even co-starring with Laurel and Hardy in 'A-Haunting We Will Go'. But as the 1950s dawned and television sounded the variety halls' death knell, stage magic and illusion declined in popularity. Mark Wilson and Doug Henning popularized television magic in America and Canada, while David Nixon, Tommy Cooper and, later, Paul Daniels did likewise on English screens.

Magicians responded by returning to their roots. If the audiences wouldn't come to them, then they would go to their audiences.

And thus the close-up magic boom was born. Canadian magician Dai Vernon, known as 'The Professor', was instrumental in this revolution. Magicians began to appear at formal dinners, wandering from table to table. They entertained on cruise liners, they graced the booths of multinational corporations at trade shows and continued to appear, as their forbears had done, on street corners and in market places.

The tricks that you are about to learn belong to this world of close-up magic. As you learn to perform them, you will be following a tradition that is thousands of years old.

1

beginnings

Proficiency in any craft requires dedication to the three 'P's – Practice, Practice and more Practice. Magic is no exception. Even though many magic tricks are actually very simple, you must practise each one until you are familiar with exactly how they work. Only by analyzing the mechanics behind an effect or routine, by seeing for yourself how your audience will view it, and by establishing what can and no doubt will go wrong, can you later perform that routine smoothly and with confidence. And the only way to achieve all that is to practise until you know the routine backwards.

Confident, well paced patter is a must, so work at developing entertaining and original narratives to accompany your routines. To aid your presentation write down what you are going to say, learn it and rehearse it. Remember that the secret of any successful performance lies in timing and pace. Having taken on board this important point let's look now at magical performance.

THE THree 'M'S OF MMMαGIC!

When performing magic there are three important 'M's that you must keep constantly in mind.

Misdirection

is the most important ingredient of any magic effect. Without it you are going to be found out, make no mistake. It basically means making the audience look where you want them to look and to perceive only what you want them to perceive. If, for example, your left hand is empty, but you are trying to convince your audience you are holding something in it, you must look at your left hand and act as though you are holding something in it. Misdirection can also involve drawing attention away from where the trickery is taking place. It can be the patter you use to relax an audience and make them take notice of you, rather than of your hands. As you practise each effect, you must isolate the moments when you are most vulnerable to exposure and learn to use misdirection to minimize the risk.

Motivation

is the art of convincing your audience you are not doing anything suspicious, when in fact you are. Whenever you perform a suspicious movement, you must give your audience a reason for it. Suppose you have something hidden in your hand that you wish to dispose of. Obviously, if you go straight to your pocket, the audience becomes suspicious. So you give them a reason for your action. You reach into your pocket, take out a pen, a coin, a box of matches or even a magic wand and in doing so, ditch the hidden object.

Moment

In any effect there are two important moments: the moment when the magic actually takes place, and the moment when the audience perceives it to have taken place. The greater the interval between the two, the greater the final impact on the audience. As you practise each routine, you must analyze exactly when these two moments occur. It is also imperative to convince your audience that something magical is happening at the perceived moment, by snapping your fingers, waving your wands or chanting your favourite magic spell.

WhAt's IN a name?

Magic

The Greeks, both impressed and mystified by the knowledge and rituals of the priestly followers of the Persian prophet Zoroaster, named them *magos*, literally meaning sorcerer, from which the adjective *magikos* was derived. The phrase *magike tekhne*, meaning sorcerers' art, craft, skill or technique, was used to describe their supposed ability to summon spirits and foretell the future. Magos passed into Latin as *magus* (plural *magi*), which in turn became *magica*. Combined with the Old French word *magique*, it evolved into English as Magick, from which the modern word magic is evolved.

The medieval magicians were academics who studied the occult arts and were believed to possess strange and wondrous powers. A word used to describe one of their activities was:

Conjure

Nathan Bailey's English Dictionary, published in 1721, defines a conjuror as 'one who is supposed to practise the vile arts of raising spirits and conferring with the Devil'. The word itself was derived from the Old French com meaning together, and the Latin *jurare* meaning to swear. From the 14th to the 18th centuries, no sleight-of-hand performer who valued his life would dare call himself a conjuror. Had he done so, he would have found himself in serious trouble, since the penalties for such a claim included being burnt at the stake. With the dawning of the Age of Reason in the 18th century, the word gradually came to be used to describe sleight-of-hand performers. Until the 18th century, those who performed sleight of hand and whom we today describe as magicians or conjurors were known as:

Jugglers

The word juggle was derived from the Latin *jocular*, itself a derivative of *jocus* from which we get the word joke. This in turn passed into Old French as *jogleur*, which was assimilated into English in the 12th century and came to denote a general entertainer. Its association with sleight of hand probably led to its later meaning, of someone who keeps several objects in the air at the same time.

There was also a class of performer busily making use of the knowledge derived from alchemists' experiments. Chaucer mentions them in *The Franklin's Tale*, referring to them as:

Tregetours

Chaucer confesses to never having actually seen their wonders, only having heard about them, but if he is to be believed it would seem that the tregetours' use of mechanical devices, optics and acoustics made them akin to our modern stage illusionists. The word itself came from the Old French *trasgeter*, which meant to pass, or to throw across.

By the 16th century, sleight of hand had also become known as:

Legerdemain

This is an Anglicized version of the French *leger de main*, meaning simply light of hand.

In the 19th century, another word came into vogue to describe the magician's art:

Prestidigitation

Specifically used to describe sleight of hand, the word is attributed to French magician Jules de Rovere who, in 1815, combined the Latin words *praestus*, meaning nimble and *digitus*, meaning finger.

2

mAgic with CARdS

Card magic was a relatively late arrival in the magician's repertoire, but it is now perhaps the most performed of all branches of the conjuror's art. In this section you will learn how to handle a deck of cards, how to secretly learn the identity of a card and how to then 'force' a spectator to take that card. After this you will learn several effects that are real audience bafflers, all of which are simple to perform.

HANDLING THE CARDS

Before attempting any card magic, it is essential that you feel comfortable when holding the deck. Although this may seem an obvious point, you may be surprised to find how ham-fisted you can become in front of an audience several of whom are watching your hands intently. A laid back, comfortable approach will not only enhance your credibility in the eyes of your audience, but will also increase your confidence.

The Standard Dealer's Grip

This is perhaps the most comfortable and relaxed way to hold your cards. The deck rests on your left hand, held in place by your fingers, with your left thumb on top.

To deal the cards, your left thumb pushes them, one by one, over to your right thumb where your right fingers grip them and deal them onto the table. Practise dealing in this way until your movements are smooth and co-ordinated.

Misdirecting the Audience One of the best methods to misdirect your audience is to make them feel relaxed in your company, and the use of humour is an excellent way to do this. A simple gag that often gets a laugh is to hand the deck of cards to a spectator and say 'shuffle those cards for me'. Before they get the chance to do anything, however, you take the deck back observing 'that's enough'.

SHUFFLING

The riffle shuffle

This is a popular shuffle but requires practice in order to perform the riffle with panache and confidence. You'll probably find that the cards will go everywhere on your first attempt. But, with perseverance, you'll soon master the move and find that your dexterity with the deck impresses your audience no end.

Cut the pack into two, gripping the top half in your right hand and the bottom half in your left. Hold the upper edge of each half with your thumbs, pressing your index finger against the backs while the other fingers hold the lower edges. Turn both halves face down, pressing the thumb edges against one another.

Begin to riffle the cards, allowing the two halves to mix together so that the individual cards become interlaced.

Having finished the riffle, straighten the cards and simply push the two halves together. With the deck now shuffled, and your audience suitably impressed, you can then proceed to astonish them further with any number of card effects.

PLAYiNg CARdS – the DeVil's PlAYthiNgs No one is really sure where playing cards came from. The records of ancient Greece and Rome make no reference to anything like them. The first mention of them in Europe comes from a 14th-century German monk named Johannes, who wrote that 'a game called the game of cards has come to us in this year 1377.' This has led to several theories about their origins. Some maintain that the Knights Templar brought them into Europe, having learned of them from the Saracens during the Crusades. Others claim that they came from either India or China after the opening of trade routes with Asia Minor and the Far East. Whichever theory is true, their appeal was unintentionally given a boost by St Bernard of Sienna, who in 1423 preached that they were the invention of the Devil. Needless to say, such sentiments increased their popularity no end! However, the cost of early playing cards made them far too expensive for wandering entertainers, and it wasn't until the 16th century, when mass-produced cards had come into general use, that jugglers were able to add a few basic card tricks to their repertoire.

The OVeRhANd ShuFF1e

This is perhaps the best known and most attempted of all card shuffles. Whereas it is simplicity itself to perform, in practice you will often find that it is easy to drop individual cards or, horror of horrors, the entire deck! So practising the essential moves until they become second nature is imperative.

Hold the deck in your left hand, with cards' faces resting on your curled fingers. Press your thumb firmly against the backs of the cards and grip the deck with your right hand.

Draw small packets of cards from the front section of the deck with your right hand, and transfer them to the back. Repeat this until you are confident that the cards are shuffled.

CUTTING THE DECK

Many of the card routines that you are going to learn will require either yourself or a spectator to cut the deck. Essentially this involves removing a packet of cards from the top of the pack and placing the section below the 'cut' onto the top, known as 'completing the cut'. You must familiarize yourself with the mechanics behind the cut, since, with many effects, you need to be able to control exactly how you do it.

1

Either place the deck on the table or hold it in you left hand ready to perform the cut. For clarity we have placed a large X on the top card to illustrate its progress. The move you are about to perform is, in essence, extremely simple, but should be practised over and over again until you become fully conversant with exactly how the deck cuts. Keep in mind that it will often be necessary for you to control exactly *how* a spectator cuts the deck.

2

With your right hand, lift any number of cards from the top of the pack. This is the actual 'cut'. Place the lower portion of the deck on top and you have completed the cut. The moves should be repeated over and over again. Try cutting near the top of the deck and complete the cut. Repeat, but cut near the bottom this time. Practise doing it both on a table and with the cards held in your hand.

LEARNING A CARD'S identity

Your audience is often much less suspicious if you allow one of them to shuffle the cards. Of course, if they do so, you have no way of knowing the position of any card. Or do you? The best and easiest way to learn the identity of the top card is to play upon your audience's natural suspicions. When the deck has been shuffled, turn the cards face up, fan them and say, 'Just make sure they're all different.' As you do, simply note and remember the top card. Cheeky, isn't it?

There you have the basics of card magic. I suggest that you take some time to re-read and work through each of them until you know them inside out. Once you are fully acquainted with each move and can execute each step smoothly and without hesitation you are ready to perform some truly astonishing card magic.

forcing a card

In many card tricks you need to make a spectator choose a particular card whilst making it appear that they had a free choice. This piece of subterfuge is known as 'forcing' and there are various methods. The important thing is to be confident in your approach. You must convince your audience that you are a decent and ethical performer not some charlatan who has made them choose a card and then pretended not to know its identity!

The cut force

At first glance this method may seem far too obvious to fool anyone. But with the correct timing and misdirection it is a tried and tested method of forcing a card upon an unsuspecting spectator. Performed with a confident and unhesitating approach it can leave your audience totally baffled.

1

This is one of those effects that are greatly enhanced by a slow paced delivery. Since it is your conversational skills that will later provide the misdirection by which you will achieve the desired result, you must accustom your audience to your talking to them from the outset. As you begin your performance allow your pace to be slow but deliberate. Place the deck upon the table with the card you wish to force on the top. In our example it is the King of Diamonds. Invite a member of your audience to step forward and cut the deck wherever they wish.

2

When they have done so, ask them if they are happy that you had no control whatsoever as to where they cut the deck. Since you didn't, they will agree that this is indeed the case. Although not strictly necessary, it is always good to get your 'volunteer' to answer questions such as this in the affirmative. You now complete the cut by placing what was the lower section of the pack on top but at an angle. Don't draw attention to what you are doing; just keep talking to emphasize the randomness of what has taken place.

3

This reassurance places distance and conversation between the cutting of the deck and the revealing of the card. You are directing your spectator's thoughts and memory away from what you have actually done. From this point on they will remember what you say you did, not what you actually did. Allow a little time to pass and then reach over and lift off the angled upper portion. Point to the top card of the lower section and ask your spectator to take their chosen card. Since this card is the original top card (the King of Diamonds) you know its identity and can reveal it however you wish.

The TURN OVER AND cut DEEPER fORCE

The following is one of my favourite methods of forcing a particular card. It's clean, direct and leaves your audience totally mystified as to how you could have known the chosen card. The great thing about this force is that, as far as your audience is concerned, you never touched the cards so could have no way of influencing them.

Have a spectator give the deck a 'thorough' shuffle. Take the cards back and, turning them face up, ask the spectator to 'make sure that all of them are different'. As you are doing this simply note and remember the top card (the King of Diamonds in our example). The audience will remember only that it was a spectator who shuffled the deck and then confirmed that all the cards were mixed.

Place the cards on the table and ask your spectator to cut the deck approximately a quarter of the way down and turn the cut pack of cards face up. As you can see from the picture the original top card (the King of Diamonds) is now the bottom card of the cut and turned over pack. Have the spectator place this face up pack on top of the remainder of the deck.

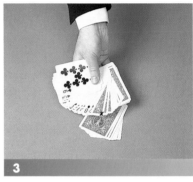

Ask the spectator to repeat the turn-over but this time to 'please cut approximately three-quarters of the way down, just to make it more random'. The force card (the King of Diamonds) is now the first face down card in the deck (for clarity we have marked it with an X in the picture). Have them replace this new packet on top of the deck exactly as they did in step two.

WAtch YOUR SPEllINg – WIZARd Originally a Wizard was a wise man and the word was used to denote a 'philosopher' or 'sage' with no suggestion of magical practices. In the Middle Ages, however, the distinction between Magic and Philosophy became somewhat blurred and by the 16th Century the prevailing definition of 'magician' and performer of magical feats had emerged.

4

Pick up the cards and emphasise to your audience that it was the spectator, not you, who shuffled them. Furthermore, point out that it was they who cut the deck, not once but twice. Get the spectator to acknowledge that they had a free choice and that you had no control over where the pack was cut. Spread out the cards and ask the spectator to take the first face down card in the deck to which they cut. It will, of course, be the force card (the King of Diamonds) and you can now reveal its identify in any way you wish.

now you see it – The first recorded magical performance

Cheops (who built the Great Pyramid) learnt from his son of a magician named Dedi who had the power to restore decapitated heads to their bodies. The King summoned this wizard to perform before him and, realizing that all magicians need an assistant, kindly offered to behead a prisoner for Dedi's trademark routine. The magician informed his monarch that the laws of nature forbade him to conjure with men, and struck a compromise by beheading a goose instead. The unfortunate bird's body was placed at one end of the hall, and its head at the other. Dedi uttered an incantation and '...the goose began to hop forward, the head moved onto it and... the goose began to cackle.'

Cheops and his amazed courtiers called for more, causing Dedi to break a major rule of the magician's code and repeat the trick, not once, but twice, albeit using a duck and an ox for his encores!

The 'decapitation illusion', as it is known today, is constantly referred to in written records of the Middle Ages, and still astonishes audiences the world over.

The routines

premonition

I've always enjoyed this routine, which relies for its effect on bold, confident presentation. A spectator freely shuffles the deck then deals any card. Despite this seemingly random process of selection, you are able to show that you knew in advance which card they would deal.

YOU WILL NEED
An ordinary deck of cards from which you have removed one (in the example, the Five of Clubs)
A duplicate of the removed card with a different coloured back (in the example, the duplicate card has a red back)
An envelope.

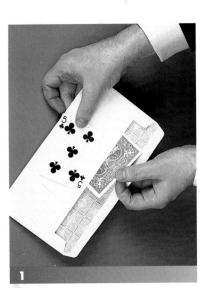

1

Having removed your 'premonition' card from the blue backed deck (in our example it is the Five of Clubs), place the duplicate card (the red backed five of clubs) into an envelope and position the removed card against the back of the envelope.

2

Put the envelope into your pocket, ensuring that the blue backed Five of Clubs is hidden behind it in such a way as to be easily, though secretly, accessible later.

3

Ask your spectator to shuffle the cards, and then deal them quickly onto the table and to stop whenever they choose. It is important that the cards are dealt untidily, so if the pile appears too neat once they have finished just casually mess the cards up a little.

Now, point out that the spectator has shuffled and dealt the cards, and that you have had nothing to do with it. 'However,' you continue, 'although I have not interfered, I have in my pocket a prediction which may, or may not, prove interesting.' Reach into your inside pocket and remove the envelope, clipping the hidden card against it. Make sure that the audience does not see it.

Drop the envelope and the card onto the dealt pile so that the Five of Clubs ends up on top. Point to the envelope and ask the spectator to pick it up.

As the spectator removes the Five of Clubs from the envelope, reach for the top card of the dealt pile saying, 'And this is the card at which you chose to stop.' Turn it over to reveal that you did, indeed, manage to predict which card they would stop at.

WAtch yOUR SpelliNG. ABRACAdABRA   It's always good to cast a spell at the moment your audience believes the magic to be taking place. Perhaps the most famous magicians' utterance is abracadabra. It has its origins in the Greek word *abrasadabra* and was used in the 2nd century by a Gnostic sect known as the Basilides when seeking help from their supreme deity abrasax. The c in the English is probably the result of a misinterpretation, since the letter c in the Greek alphabet stands for s.

The TRiA1 OF The cenTuRY

Forcing a spectator to choose a particular card can also be done verbally using a method known as 'The Magician's Choice'. Basically, it gives the spectator no choice at all. The key to this particular force is a confident and unhesitant delivery.

1

Place the force card on top of the deck (in our example, the Queen of Diamonds) and explain, 'There are four suits in a deck of cards – Diamonds, Hearts, Spades and Clubs – do you agree?' The spectator will, of course, agree.

Ask your spectator to imagine that you are holding the red suits in your right hand, and the black in your left, then ask, 'Which shall I put down, the red or the black?' It is important to ask for a choice between red and black, because many people will name a suit rather than a colour.

Now begins the force. If the spectator chooses red, say, 'Good choice, then we shall use the red.' If they choose black, put the imaginary black suits down and say, 'Good choice, then we shall use the red suits that I hold in my hands!' Are you getting the idea now?

Continue by saying, 'There are two red suits, Hearts and Diamonds. Name one.' If the choice is Diamonds, say, 'Then Diamonds it is.' If Hearts are chosen, say, 'Fine, then I get to use my favourite suit – Diamonds.'

2

So you've forced the spectator to choose Diamonds. All that now remains for you to do is to force a 'free choice' of the card you have already chosen – the Queen of Diamonds. My own preference is to turn the trick into a trial, with the spectator playing the part of a judge. 'Let's add a little excitement, a little danger. Please hold your hand over the deck. Imagine you're a judge, and appearing before you are...' (hesitate here as though thinking) '...let's say the King and Queen of Diamonds. You must execute one and you hold the hand of protection over the other. Which will you execute and over which do you extend the hand of protection?'

If they choose to execute the Queen say, 'So the Queen dies. Please turn over the top card.' If they choose to execute the King say, 'So you hold the hand of protection over the Queen. You want her to live?' When they agree, say, 'Then please turn over the top card.' Of course in both instances your spectator's 'freely chosen' card is on top.

now you see it. **Biblical Sorcery** The Bible is full of references to magical performances and happenings. When Moses and Aaron appeared before Pharaoh urging him to 'Let my people go', Aaron threw down his rod, turning it into a serpent. Despite the duplication of the feat by Pharaoh's 'magicians', Aaron demonstrated his magical superiority by having his serpent swallow theirs.

When Ahab, worried by a prolonged drought, ordered a competition between the magicians of Baal and the Lord's representative, Elijah, the former faction failed to meet the latter's challenge to call down fire from heaven. As his performance began, determined not to be accused of trickery, Elijah had a trench dug around his altar, filled it with water and doused not only the sacrificial bullock but also the wood which was to be used to burn it. Having gone through this Scriptural equivalent of showing 'nothing up my sleeve', he then caused the fire of the Lord to fall and consume the burnt sacrifice and the wood. Elijah had won the world's first recorded Magic Competition and, rather unsportingly, promptly slew his rival magicians!

come fouRth

The following is little more than an old fairground swindle but is one of those tricks that offers a delightful twist. Again the spectator seems to have a totally free choice of any card, but actually picks the card that you have forced them to take. However, you appear at first to have got the card wrong, much to the spectator's glee. Having allowed them a few moments to gloat at your apparent misfortune you then turn the tables. This type of routine is, for obvious reasons, known as a 'sucker' effect.

Pick the deck and cut it into four approximately equal piles. It is imperative that you ensure that the portion cut from the top of the pack, that is the one containing the Ten of Diamonds, is in the far right pile, as you look at it. We have reversed the force card in the picture for clarity.

Hand the cards to your spectator and ask them to give the deck a thorough shuffle. Taking them back, begin to deal cards face up onto the table. As you do so remember the fourth card dealt, in our example the Ten of Diamonds. It's a good idea to repeat the name of the fourth card quietly to yourself several times to help you remember it.

Don't hesitate at this card. Just deal a few more cards on top of it before saying, 'Tell me when to stop.' Gather up the dealt cards and replace them on the remainder of the deck, so that the fourth card down is still the Ten of Diamonds.

Taking the cards back, begin dealing them face up. When the force card is dealt, don't react or acknowledge it; just keep dealing cards onto it, ensuring that it protrudes slightly. After a few more cards, pause, and indicating the card you are about to deal, announce, 'the next card I turn over will be the card you saw!' Since the correct card is protruding from the dealt pile, the spectator will be emphatic that you are wrong – even confident enough to make a small wager!

Pointing to the far right pile, ask your spectator to take the top card and place it on the far left pile. The next card is to go on the pile second from the left. The third card goes onto the pile next to the force pile. This now leaves the Ten of Diamonds (marked with an X in our example) on top of the force pile. Ask your spectator to pick up this card, remember it, replace it in any pile, gather all the cards together and shuffle the deck.

Give your spectator ample time to gloat at your obvious mistake. They will often tell you in no uncertain terms that you are definitely wrong. Of course they haven't listened to your exact claim that the 'next card' you turn over will be their card. When you feel ready to turn the tables, reach to the dealt cards and turn over the Ten of Diamonds.

DiviNiNg The cARds

Another popular magicians' ruse is known as the 'one ahead principle'. The following routine, in which you name the top cards of four freely cut piles, without actually knowing their identities beforehand, is an excellent example of the mechanics behind this extremely useful principle.

1

Have a spectator shuffle the cards. Retrieve the deck and, fanning them face up, ask the spectator to confirm that the cards are all different. As you do so, note and remember the top card. In our example, it is the Jack of Hearts.

2

Divide the deck into four approximately equal piles, with the original top card (marked with an X in the picture) on the far right.

Look at the top card on the far left pile, pretend to concentrate and predict confidently that it will be the Jack of Hearts. Pick the card up, without allowing the audience to see it, nod and smile. As you can see from the picture, the card is actually the Seven of Hearts, but you are now in the 'one ahead' position. Once you have miscalled the identity of this card, move quickly on.

3

Reaching for the next pile, announce 'Seven of Hearts', (as you can see in the picture, it is the Two of Diamonds), look at it as you pick it up, and nod.

4

Reach for the next pile and announce 'Two of Diamonds', again nod smugly (it is actually the Ten of Diamonds) and, reaching to the final pile, announce 'Ten of Diamonds' (it is of course the Jack of Hearts).

5

As you add this card to the others, place it behind the Seven of Hearts, thus ensuring that the order is exactly as you called it. Show the cards to your spectator to demonstrate that you successfully 'divined the cards'.

TRue mAgiC – whAt the AudieNCe thiNKs they see

When rehearsing any of the magic routines in this book never forget that *True magic* does not happen in the magician's hands, it happens in the spectator's mind. That is why you will seldom find me describing any of the routines as 'tricks'. They are and must be presented as 'effects'. You must see yourself as an actor playing the part of a magician and, just as great actors analyse the character they are assuming and allow that character to live through them, so must you allow the effects and routines to assume a life of their own through you.

fOllOW The LeadeR

Four Ace effects are a very popular form of card magic and there are many effects in which the aces 'magically' come together under seemingly impossible conditions. In this routine, you have the aces lost in the deck, but with a few mystical incantations, cause them to be re-united. I suggest you practise in front of a mirror until you are confident with the required concealment that makes the effect possible.

1

Out of sight of your spectators remove four like cards from the deck. Although our example uses the aces it can be any four you wish. Also remove three other cards (we've chosen the Seven, Eight and Nine of Clubs). Put the three other cards (the Clubs) behind three of the Aces, and place the remaining ace (in our example the Ace of Spades) behind the Clubs. Since any card in the wrong order will adversely affect the outcome of the effect always check that your cards are correctly set prior to your performance.

2

Fan the seven cards so that the three Clubs are hidden between the Aces and show them to your spectators. Once you have shown the fan, place the seven cards that the spectators believe to be just four Aces onto the top of the deck. The actual order is: one Ace (the Ace of Spades) followed by the three other cards, followed by the three remaining Aces.

3

Taking the top card (the Ace of Spades), place it face up on the table and ask if your audience have ever played 'Follow the Leader'. Pointing to the face-up card say, 'If I place this Ace here the other three...' (point to the deck in your hand) '... become eager to join it. I can feel them struggling to escape, I'd better confine them.' Remove the cards one at a time from the top (we've put an X on them) and place them into the deck. What you have actually done is lose the three indifferent cards, leaving the three aces on top.

4

As far as the audience is concerned, you have inserted the three Aces into the deck. Continue with the saga. 'Of course, the poor old Ace of Spades has now lost its three closest friends and is beginning to feel very lonely indeed. Let's give it three new friends to keep it company.' As you say this begin counting the three top cards of the deck (which are actually the Aces) face down onto the face-up Ace of Spades. It's a good idea to angle the deck down slightly so there is no danger of you flashing the faces of the cards as you deal and giving the game away prematurely.

5

Pause as you deal the final Ace and say, 'The funny thing is that cards will, somehow, always follow their leader.' Turn over the three Aces to show that, indeed, the Aces have been reunited. You are now, in magicians' parlance, 'clean'. Everything can be examined without giving any clue as to how you achieved the end result.

MAgNetic HANds

It is an old cliché that the hand is quicker than the eye. It's also completely untrue, for the eye is virtually impossible to deceive. Unfortunately the same cannot be said for the brain, which has the unenviable task of interpreting all the images presented to it by the eye. Optical illusions depend very much on how the mind perceives – or to be more precise, misperceives – what the eye sees. Confused? Try the following routine on an unsuspecting spectator, and you'll begin to grasp a basic principle of magic and illusion – that a huge void exists between sight and perception.

1 Remove the Eights and Nines of Spades and Clubs from the deck. Place the Eight of Spades with the Nine of Clubs and the Nine of Spades with the Eight of Clubs and prepare to both baffle and astound your audience.

2 Place the Nine of Spades on the bottom of the deck, the Eight of Clubs on the top and lay the other two cards face down on the table. Pick up the Nine of Clubs and Eight of Spades, keeping them face down. Ask your audience, 'Did you know that you can now buy magnetic decks of cards?' Chances are that this will be a total revelation, but even if it isn't, what you say next will be. 'I only discovered this after going for cosmetic surgery to have magnets implanted in my fingertips.'

3 Offer to demonstrate your magnetic fingers and, without drawing attention to the actual suits of the two cards, simply flash them at the spectator, just long enough for the values to register.

Turn the two cards face down, pick up the deck and push the cards into it.

The top and bottom cards of the deck are, of course, the corresponding cards to the two you have just disposed of. Gripping the deck firmly, give it a sudden and violent shake, causing all the cards except those on the top and bottom to scatter untidily.

Tip – performing magic

It is important that, whenever, you are performing a feat of magic you treat your audience with respect. Always be nice and always be humble. The only difference between you and your audience is that you have learnt to do something that they haven't. Never belittle a spectator or think yourself better than them. No one likes a Clever Dick and remember the old adage 'Pride Comes before a fall'. You never know when or where you'll meet those spectators again. Today's humiliated spectators might be tomorrow's in-laws!

Hold up the two cards that you now hold in your fingers, and it will appear to your audience that you have managed to retain the two cards you showed them earlier. Look amazed and say, 'It's all done with magnets.'

Like finds Like

The final routine in this section is an excellent example of a 'self-working' effect. Although these are often very simple to perform, with good presentation you can both astonish and baffle your audience. The great thing about this type of effect is that it will work despite every effort by the spectator to change the outcome.

Arrange the Aces and court cards into their respective suits and deal them face up into four rows. Gather them together row by row and ask the spectator to cut the cards four times. It doesn't matter how many cards each cut contains, and it's a good idea to emphasize this apparent choice.

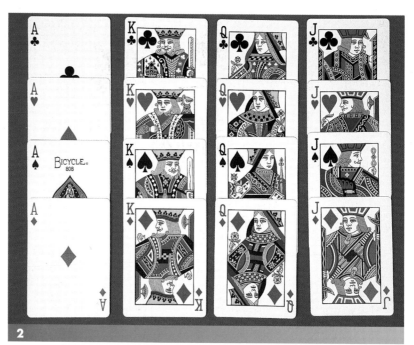

Take the cards back (you can pick up the four piles from either left to right or right to left, but not randomly). Deal them into four rows, but this time from left to right. The cards will now appear to have arranged themselves by value as opposed to by suit. Gather them together and ask the spectator to again cut the packet four times. Deal them one at a time from top to bottom and the cards will appear to have rearranged themselves back into their complete suits.

The beauty of this simple, self-working effect is that you can do it as many times as you like, over and over again.

money magic

Ever since money was first used as a means of exchange, people have been devising ways of making it disappear. Magicians invented numerous routines to vanish a spectator's coin and, sometimes, make it reappear in the most unexpected places. Money magic is still popular today, and one of the first magic routines most people ever see is someone pulling a coin out of their ear. In this chapter you'll learn several clever vanishes as well as some cruel and ingenious stunts to perform with borrowed coins or notes.

a simple coin vanish

Causing small objects such as coins to vanish, apparently into thin air, is one of the best-known forms of close-up magic. There are many ways of achieving this, and the following routine is one of the easiest. Although the basic moves are simple, a confident and smooth approach is essential.

YOU WILL NEED
A handkerchief
A coin.

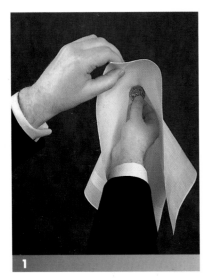

1

Holding the handkerchief in your left hand and the coin in your right, drape the handkerchief gradually over the coin until the coin is positioned in the middle of the handkerchief.

2

Having twisted the handkerchief around the coin, hold it with your right hand and pinch the coin through the fabric with your left fingers. This is emphasising that the coin is actually there. Repeat step one and this pinching action a few times to condition your audience to the idea that the coin always ends up at the centre of the handkerchief.

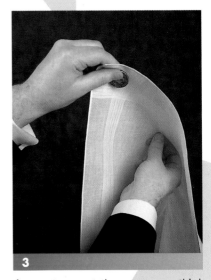

3

Appear to repeat the sequence a third time but as you begin to do so, switch the coin from your right to left hand, clipping it to the underside of the handkerchief with your left thumb. Without hesitating, continue to slide your right fingers to the centre as though they still hold the coin.

5

Blow on the handkerchief and, with a quick shake, allow it to fall free – showing that the coin has, apparently, vanished. The handkerchief provides ample cover for the hidden coin.

4

Allow the handkerchief to drape over your fingers but act as though you still have the coin at the centre. Pinch the now empty handkerchief with the fingers of your left hand just as you did in step two. Practice this since you will need to ensure you apply only enough pressure to create the impression you are gripping a coin. Too much pressure and the handkerchief will collapse exposing the trickery.

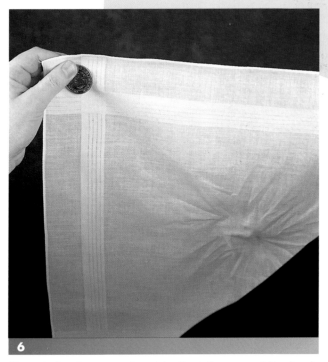

6

The coin is of course, clipped to the left corner of the handkerchief held in place by your left thumb and fingers. You can shake the handkerchief about a few times to show that the coin has actually vanished, then screw it up (being careful not to expose the coin) and deposit it into a convenient pocket.

a Bold Coin Vanish

The brazen method employed in this very simple coin vanish can, with practice and timing, leave your audience totally baffled. Borrow a coin and display it between your left-hand thumb and first finger. Turning to the spectator say, 'Is this the coin that you just gave me?' When they agree say, 'Thank you very much', and placing it in your pocket say, 'Let's do a card trick'.

2

Using the tips of your fingers, brush the coin underneath your raised foot and at the same time close your fingers as though you have picked up the coin.

3

You will need to practise the moves to ensure that your actions are both smooth and convincing. Your audience must believe that you have taken the coin.

1

Of course the unimpressed spectator will request the return of their coin. Pretending to relent, take out their coin, but accidently drop it. Say 'Butterfingers' and stoop down to pick it up. As you do so raise the toe of your right foot slightly.

4

Straighten up, pretending that you are actually holding the coin in your clenched fist. Ask your spectator to hold out their hand and, as they do so, blow upon your fist, then open it to show that their coin has mysteriously vanished into thin air.

The MYSTERIOUS COIN VANish

In the following routine, you will make use of a hidden coin, that the spectator will be unaware of, to achieve a truly remarkable effect. You will cause a coin that is, apparently, always in the spectator's possession to vanish out of their hand. What could be more magical or astonishing than that?

YOU WILL NEED

Two identical handkerchiefs

A needle and thread

A pair of scissors

Two coins of the same value (one of which can be borrowed)

A pen, which you keep in an inside pocket.

1

First, you need to construct your 'gimmick'. Lay a coin on the top right corner of one handkerchief, cut a small square of fabric from the duplicate and sew this square over the coin. Place the pen in an inside pocket and you're ready to perform.

2

Hold the handkerchief by its corners in such away that your fingers are over the hidden coin and either borrow or give a coin of equal value from or to your spectator. Ask them to examine the coin to 'make sure it's normal'.

3

Draping the handkerchief over your cupped left fist, fold its corners into your clenched palm using your right hand. Practise this to ensure that you can do it swiftly and smoothly and in such a way that doesn't draw attention to the gimmicked corner.

4

Ask your spectator to drop their coin into 'this little investment portfolio, to see if we can increase its value'. Don't give them the chance to push it too far in, since they may feel the gimmick. The moment the coin is in your fist, grip it with the your right hand thumb and fingers and immediately turn your left hand over.

5

Under cover of the handkerchief, push the gimmicked coin upwards and ask the spectator to hold their coin through the fabric. At the same time allow their actual coin to drop into the palm of your right hand. You have ample cover to get a decent grip on the coin. Practise until you can perform the move smoothly.

6

Ask your spectator to keep hold of their coin and twist it through the handkerchief. As they do so say, 'I will need a pen for this.' Reach into your pocket ostensibly to remove a pen but actually to dispose of the coin.

Gesturing with the pen inform your audience that 'money is a fickle friend, it's easy to make but difficult to hold on to'. Pause and ask your spectator if they can feel the coin. The spectator will say 'yes'. As the rest of the audience sees it the spectator is confirming that the coin is still present. Continue, 'But at that moment when you think you have money...' (again ask your spectator if they can feel it) '... it turns out to be nothing more than a cruel, though effective illusion'. As you say this snatch the handkerchief from the spectator's grip and shake it to show that the coin has vanished.

The COIN fold VANish

This is a simple but fiendishly deceptive method of vanishing a coin from inside a square of paper that has been folded around it. Once you have mastered the basic technique you can adapt it to create all manner of astonishing and seemingly impossible coin vanishing routines.

YOU WILL NEED

A 13 cm (5 inch) square of paper

A borrowed coin.

1

Place a coin at the centre of your square of paper and inform your audience that you wish to wrap the coin to protect it.

2

Fold the lower quarter of the paper up over the coin.

3

Fold the right side back behind the coin, while keeping the coin in place with your thumb.

fANCY thAt ... OOpS! Conjurors have been performing tricks with coins for hundreds, if not thousands of years, sometimes with alarming results. On 3rd April 1843 the great Victorian engineer Isambard Kingdom Brunel (1806–1859), a keen amateur magician, was entertaining his children by placing a coin into his ear and then removing it from his mouth. Unfortunately he accidently swallowed the duplicate coin hidden inside his mouth and it stuck in his throat where, despite the attempts of eminent surgeons it stayed for several weeks. Having almost choked to death, Brunel had himself strapped to a wooden board and pinioned between two upright poles. He was then spun round at great speed, the centrifugal force of which finally dislodged the coin.

Fold the left side back behind the coin.

Now fold the remainder down behind the coin, leaving the coin sitting in a loose pocket. The fold should be completed without hesitation, giving your audience the impression that the coin is secure inside the small paper packet.

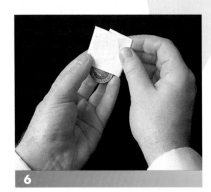

Transfer the packet to your left hand and, while giving the impression of creasing the folds, turn it over so that the opening is pointing down into your curled fingers. If you loosen your grip slightly, the coin will now slip from the packet and drop unseen into your hand.

Transfer the empty packet back to your right hand.

With your left hand, reach into your inside pocket to remove a pen, a wand, a box of matches – whatever you please. Of course as you do so, you simply ditch the coin and free yourself to tear, burn or even crumple up the paper packet, showing that the coin has mysteriously vanished.

COiN THROUGH COASTER

Having become fully conversant with the Coin Fold Vanish, you can now perform this astonishing routine in which you apparently cause a borrowed coin to penetrate through a coaster and drop into a glass tumbler. This delightful and astonishing effect will have your audience convinced that you can truly work magic upon everyday objects.

YOU WILL NEED

A coaster

A clear glass tumbler

A borrowed coin

A sticky label.

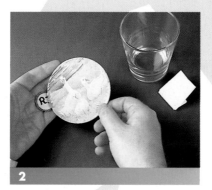

1 Having borrowed a coin, ask your spectator to initial a label then stick it onto the coin, so that they can identify it as theirs should they 'be fortunate enough to see it again'!

Perform the Coin Fold Vanish (see page 47) but retain the coin in your left hand. Having transferred the (now empty) packet to your right hand, set it down on the table and pick up the coaster.

2 With the coin hidden in your left hand, transfer the coaster into that hand in such a way that it hides the coin. Practise the timing of this move so that you are able to do it swiftly and smoothly.

3 Place the coaster over the mouth of the glass, trapping the coin in such a way that the slightest movement will cause it to overbalance. You will need to practise this move until you can do it smoothly and, most importantly, silently.

CleANliNess is Next to GodliNess Magic is very much an intrusive entertainment, by which I mean that you will often be invading your audience's personal space. By the very nature of your performance you will be touching people and they will be touching you. It's time for a long hard look in that mirror. Is the person you see staring back the sort of person you would want to be touched by? Your audience must feel relaxed by your presence not repulsed or threatened. So ensure that you and your clothing are both clean and fragrant and that your props are in pristine condition. Remember first impressions count and that most people will have decided whether or not they like you within moments of meeting you.

4

Pick up the paper packet that supposedly holds the coin, place it on the coaster and, with your index finger begin to press. You need to act as though you are actually trying to push the coin from the packet and into the glass. The more convincing you are at pretending the coin is still inside the packet, the greater the effect will be on your audience when the coin later drops into the glass.

5

A slight pressure or movement will now dislodge the coin, causing it to drop suddenly into the glass. Allow your spectator to retrieve their coin and to verify the initials. It will look to them as though you have caused their initialled coin to penetrate a solid coaster – and what could be more magical than that?

LiNKiNG PApER Clips

In this impromptu routine, which can be done with borrowed props, you cause two paper clips to link together mysteriously. Although not earth-shattering magic, it's a good quick trick to have in your repertoire. There will be occasions when you need an impromptu routine such as this to fill a gap in your performance.

YOU WILL NEED

A bank note of any denomination

2 paper clips.

Fold the note into a 'Z'.

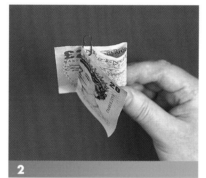

Fasten the middle section to the back section with one of the paper clips.

Fasten the opposite side of the middle section to the front section using the remaining paper clip.

5

Grip the corners of the front and back sections firmly and give them a sharp pull, causing the note to open out.

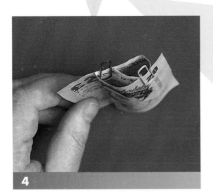

4

Your note should now be clipped like the one shown above.

6

This will cause the two paper clips to fly off the note and, as they do, the two clips will become linked together.

fANCY thAt! Ventriloquism is one of the many facets of the magical arts. The word is derived from the Latin *Venter* meaning 'stomach' and *locqui* meaning 'speak'. Its literal meaning is 'stomach-speaker' and originally referred to the phenomenon of speaking from the abdomen, a sure sign of possession by an evil spirit. It wasn't used to describe the trick of throwing ones voice until the end of the 18th century. It is a popular misconception that ventriloquists actually throw their voices, when in fact the art depends largely on misdirection. It is easier to deceive the ear than the eye and a talented performer can, by simply changing the tone of his voice and looking in a particular direction, convince an audience that the sound is coming from elsewhere.

rollover

I have been performing this routine for over twelve years and I still enjoy it. It is a delightful example of a spectator believing that you are trying to deceive them in a particular way, only to find that you have – but not quite as they had expected.

YOU WILL NEED

2 bank notes of differing values
(yours should be the one lower in value).

Arrange the notes so that yours is on top of theirs, and say 'I'll place your money on top, and my money beneath it.' Your spectator will immediately correct you and point out that theirs is on the bottom. It is important that they do so, because they must remember the order of the two notes.

Begin rolling the two notes together.

Ask your spectator to loan you a bank note of a higher value than the one you intend to use, assuring them that you intend to match it.

Once the spectator's note is on the table, place yours next to it and say, 'There you are, a perfect match.' Since your note has a lower value, the spectator will protest that it is hardly a fair match. Smile, and just carry on observing philosophically, 'Ah, but I know what will happen.'

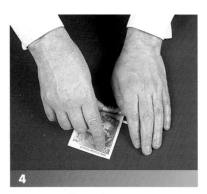

4

5

As you can see from the photograph, the left side is rolled a lot quicker than the right. This is because the actual 'magic move' happens on the left. Of course it is imperative that your spectator does not notice this, so you will need to misdirect their attention.

As the left side of your money reaches the edge of theirs, cover that corner with your left hand. Using your right hand, point to the right-hand corner of their note and say, 'Please could you hold that corner for me'. In so doing, you direct their attention away from your left hand (where the trickery is happening) and onto your right hand (where nothing important is happening).

Under the ample cover provided by your left hand, simply allow that side of the two notes to flip under and over each other. This has caused the notes to change places. Your spectator's money is now on top. Don't reveal this fact yet; rather, remind your audience of the sequence of events. 'If you remember, we placed your money on top and mine on the bottom'. Again the spectator will disagree, insisting that their money is on the bottom.

6

'In that case', you say, as you unroll the notes, 'please take your money, which you emphatically stated was on the bottom, and I shall retrieve mine from the top'. As the notes unroll, the spectator will see that you have turned the tables, and that the two notes have mysteriously changed places.

WHAT'S IN a NAME? TRICK   Oddly enough, many magicians do not like the word trick, preferring instead 'effect' or 'routine'. This could have something to do with the word's origins. It was acquired from the Old French *trique*, a divergent of *triche* from the verb *trichier* meaning to cheat, which is the source of the word treachery. So when someone asks you to 'do a trick', they are either asking you to cheat or be treacherous, and magicians are far too nice and honest to sink to such levels!

MONEY TO BURN

It is a fact of life that people often take delight in the misfortune of others, the old gag of someone slipping on a banana skin being a classic example. With this in mind, you are about to perform either one of the best (or cruellest) routines that magic can offer – you borrow a spectator's money and promptly set fire to it. Of course, being a magician, you then restore it, but not without milking the situation for all it is worth!

YOU WILL NEED
An envelope
A pair of scissors
An ashtray
A lighter or box of matches
A boxed deck of cards
A glass of water – for safety purposes
A borrowed bank note.

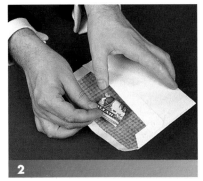

First, cut a small slit in the front (address side) of an envelope. Put the cards (with the box lid open), together with the matches or lighter, into an inside pocket. Place a large ashtray on the table and you are ready to perform.

Ask a spectator to 'lend' you the highest value bank note they can spare. Here you will discover an intriguing paradox of magic for, despite your politeness of manner and specificity of your request, you will invariably be given the lowest value bank note that the spectator possesses!

Accept it graciously, asking the spectator to 'sign your note so that you will recognize it if you see it again.' Fold it in such a way that it will fit easily through the slit in the envelope. Pick up the envelope, keeping the secret slit hidden, and slip the folded note inside.

As the money goes into the envelope, push it out through the envelope. In the picture, the hand is clear of the slit for clarity.

Keeping the spectator's money hidden in the curled fingers of your left hand, turn the envelope over so as to cover the note (for clarity the photograph shows an exposed view) and seal it.

Ask if your spectator has a light, then without giving them a chance to respond, say, 'Don't worry, I have one in my pocket.' You now have a believable reason for reaching into the pocket that contains the lighter or matches.

As you do so, jam the spectator's folded money into the open card box so that it slides between the cards. You will need to practice this until you can execute the move quickly and smoothly.

Set fire to the envelope, allowing it to burn until just ashes remain in the ashtray. Be careful and keep the glass of water on standby, just in case.

Tell your spectator not to worry, since you have, using your 'magical powers', protected their money from the flames. Ask them to sift through the ashes and retrieve their undamaged money. As they are doing this, remove your deck of cards and place it on the table.

When the bemused spectator finds no trace of their money, apologize and explain that things sometimes do go wrong. Then add, 'But you can at least draw comfort from the mirth and enjoyment your selfless generosity has given us all.' Turning to the rest of your audience, say, 'I think a round of applause is called for.'

As the applause dies down, pick up and remove the cards from the box, saying, 'Luckily, being a magician, I am able to perform a selection of card tricks, which will redeem the exact value of your lost money.' Place the cards in front of your spectator, and ask them to cut wherever they wish. Because of the thickness of the money, they will, 99.9 per cent of the time, cut to the concealed bank note.

Ask the spectator to verify that it is their signed bank note. Breathe a sigh of relief and say, 'All's well that ends well.'

clever stuff

By now you should have acquired a reasonable understanding of misdirection, motivation, moment as well as several other magical principals. In this chapter you will put this knowledge to good use, as you begin to create props and gimmicks that will help you to create some astonishing and baffling routines. As well as learning some of the great 'classics' of magic you will also begin to hone your performing abilities as you add flair and panache to your act.

DO eggsActly As I DO

A famous tale tells how, when Christopher Columbus had completed his trans-oceanic voyage of discovery and was enjoying a celebratory feast, a faction of courtiers scoffed at his achievement, telling him that anyone else could easily have accomplished such an epic voyage. Columbus countered with: 'Yes, but can anyone here balance an egg on its end?' Once his challengers had all tried and failed, he took the egg and crushed it onto the table, causing it to stand – just as he had promised – on end. The courtiers dismissed the display as an easy and childish trick. 'Yes it is,' Columbus replied, 'when you know how.'

The story, whether true or not, makes an excellent introduction to the routine that follows. You offer your audience an egg and ask them if they can balance it on end without crushing it. They will be unable to do so, yet – with a few magical words – you manage to achieve the impossible feat.

YOU WILL NEED

An ordinary egg

A white background such as a
    tablecloth or handkerchief

Salt.

1

Whilst your audience attempt to stand the egg on its end, surreptitiously conceal a small amount of salt in the palm of your hand. In the picture we have exaggerated the amount necessary. You will need to practice this routine alone several times to get an idea of the minimum amount required.

2

Leaning forward to take the egg with your right hand and allow the salt to run from your hand in such a way a that it forms a small pile that will be easily camouflaged by the white background.

4

Having uttered a few magical incantations, let go of the egg and leave it balancing, just as you promised, on its end. Again, for purposes of clarity we have exaggerated the amount of salt required in the photograph.

3

Placing the egg onto the pile of salt, twisting it a little so that it stands upright. Again you will need to practise this move alone until you know exactly how much pressure needs to be applied.

5

Leave the egg standing on its end for a little while longer, then pick it up and hand it to your audience for inspection. There may be a few telltale specks of salt on it, so push it across the table in such a way that they are removed. As the spectators inspect the egg, you can surreptitiously brush the salt away, from the tablecloth or pick up the handkerchief and place it in your pocket. Either way you've dispersed the evidence and you can end by saying, 'Now I'm off to discover America.'

The cups and Balls

This is a simple version of a true classic that must be one of the world's oldest magic routines. It was so well known in ancient Greece and Rome that the Greeks called the conjuror *psephopaiktes* from the pebbles used in this effect, while the Romans knew him as either *calcularius* from the little stones or *acetabularius* from the cups. Much later, artists such as Hieronymus Bosch and Jan Breughel painted street scenes that often included a juggler performing the Cups and Balls trick somewhere on the canvas. (Interestingly, those same scenes often show a pickpocket at work amongst the distracted audience!) Most modern magicians have a version of it in their repertoire. Well presented, it is as astonishing as it is baffling.

Below is a simplified version of this classic of close-up magic. Once you have mastered it, try exploring the plethora of magical literature to find ways of taking it to ever more mysterious heights.

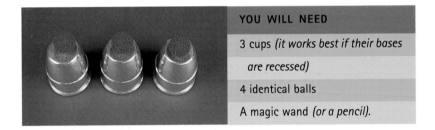

YOU WILL NEED

3 cups *(it works best if their bases are recessed)*

4 identical balls

A magic wand *(or a pencil)*.

1

Place one cup into another. Drop one ball into the second cup.

2

Place the third cup into the second (hiding the ball), and drop the remaining three balls into the third cup.

3

As you begin your performance, tip the three balls onto the table and arrange them in a line, leaving a gap between them. Remove the first cup, turn it upside down, and place it on the table behind the first ball. Do likewise with the next cup, placing it behind the middle ball, taking care not to let the audience see the ball hidden inside it. Practise this move to prevent the ball falling out.

4

Place the final cup behind the third ball and tap the bottoms of the cups with your magic wand just to show that they are solid.

5

Place one ball on top of the middle cup and nest the other cups over it.

6

Tap the stack with either your finger or your magic wand. Your intention is to give the impression that you are doing something magical that will cause the ball to penetrate the cup. Pick up the stack of cups and show that the ball has apparently passed through the cup.

7

Pick up the three cups and set them down on the table again, placing the cup with the hidden ball in it over the ball that has just penetrated the cup. Place a second ball on top of this cup and stack the cups again. Tap the top of the stack with your finger or magic wand, then lift the stack to show that another ball has magically passed through the solid cup.

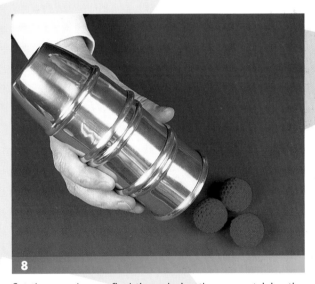

8

Set the cups down a final time, placing the cup containing the hidden ball over the two balls that have already passed through. Place the final ball over this cup and restack the cups. With one final magical tap, lift the stack to show that all three balls have now magically passed through the cup.

now you see it The first written account of a performance of the classic Cups and Balls routine is contained in an epistle by the 2nd-century Greek writer *Alciphron*, who described how he was rendered almost speechless when he saw it. Ruminating on the performer's dexterity, he commented that if he were to invite him to his farm, 'We should never be able to catch him in his tricks, and he would steal everything I had, and strip my farm of all it contains!'

The Time-TRAVelling MAtch

In this tried and tested audience baffler, you tear a match from a book of matches, light it, cause it to vanish into thin air and reappear, reconnected but burnt to a cinder, back amongst the remaining matches in the book. Read that description again because that is, word for word, precisely what you are about to do – at least as far as your audience is concerned. By now you've probably guessed that the reality is somewhat different!

YOU WILL NEED

A specially-prepared book of matches

A glass of water for safety.

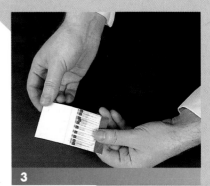

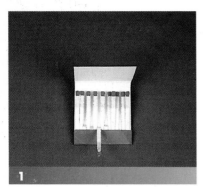

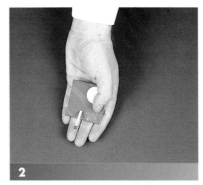

1

To prepare the match book, remove and discard some of the matches so that about ten remain. Leave a cluster of matches around the centre and bend one match forward and out of the book. Light it with one of the discarded matches and extinguish it. Take special care not to ignite the other matches and mind you don't burn your fingers.

2

Bend the remaining cluster slightly and close the flap, leaving the burnt match on the outside. You are now ready to perform the miracle of the time machine.

3

Tell your audience that after years of trying you have finally succeeded in your endeavours to construct a miniature time machine. Pick up the matchbook and, hiding the burnt match with your thumb, introduce your 'state-of-the-art time-machine'. Being careful not to flash the hidden match, open the book and show the contents.

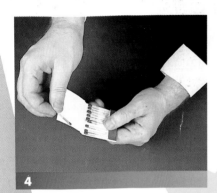

4

Have a spectator count the matches, explaining that one of them will be your time traveller. You could even add, 'I will cause it to boldly go where no match has gone before', then talk a little about infinity as you apologize for your split infinitive! Tear one from the cluster saying, 'This will do'. As you do so, push the hidden, burnt match back into the cluster with your left hand and close the book.

5

Say, 'Between any two events that happen one after the other, there is an interval that we call time. I have discovered that, if you can create enough energy and speed, it is possible to bridge that gap and literally travel through time'. As you say this, strike the match.

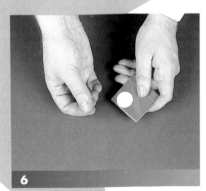

6

Shaking the match to extinguish it, say that you need to reach sufficient speed to propel it through time. Keep shaking the match to condition your audience to the movement. On a backward shake, let go of the match letting it fly over your shoulder. However, continue the shaking motion so that your audience thinks you are still in possession of the match. After a few moments give your hand a violent jerk to create the impression that *this* is the moment when the match vanishes.

7

The rest of the routine is pure acting on your part. Inform your audience that the match has now gone back in time to when the experiment began. 'Of course,' continue nonchalantly, 'one of the dangers of time travel is that anything we do in another dimension can affect us dramatically'. Open the match book to reveal the burnt match, now reconnected exactly as it was at the start of the experiment, except that it bears the physical scars of its 'encounter with its future'. You should practise this routine over and over again in front of the mirror, until your timing is such that each move convinces even you!

The LAdy VANishes

The effect that follows has a chequered history and has probably b_____ another, for as long as playing cards themselves. It is also known as either _____ The Lady. A spectator is encouraged to bet on which of three cards is the 'Lady' or Queen, but as you will see from this easy-to-perform version, the only winners are those perpetrating the scam. That said, as a harmless bit of fun, it is as baffling as it is deceitful.

YOU WILL NEED

Three playing cards

A special gimmick,
   for which you will need:

A Queen playing card

Any other playing card

A pair of scissors

Clear tape

A pencil.

1

I suggest that your three cards consist of two corresponding values from either the red or black suits. The example uses the Threes of Hearts and Diamonds. The third card is not overly important. For the gimmick you will need a Queen (Hearts in our example) and an indifferent card such as the Joker.

2

Pencil an arc across an index corner of the Queen and place this card over the Joker. (For clarity we have emphasized the mark in the picture.)

3

Cut this corner from both the Queen and the Joker.

5

Slide this gimmicked pocket over an index corner of either of the two corresponding value cards, and you're ready to perform.

6

Fan the three cards in such a way that the middle card appears to be a Queen. It is in fact the gimmicked pocket. Point out that the 'Lady' is the middle card and ask your spectator to remember this.

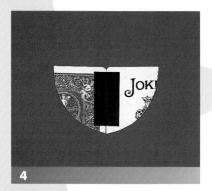

4

Laying the Queen corner face down against that of the Joker, stick the two together with a piece of clear tape. We have used black tape to emphasize it.

WHAt'S IN a NAme? Gimmick

The modern definition of the word gimmick as 'something designed to draw attention' is, when applied to magic, an oxymoron. No magician worth his salt would ever draw attention to the use of a gimmick. However, although the origin of the word is unknown, it first appeared in print in the 1926 American publication *The Wise Crack Dictionary* where it is defined as a 'device for making a fair game crooked'. It has been suggested that it began as gimac, an anagram of magic, once used by conjurors to describe their implements.

7

Turn the cards face down and ask the spectator if they can remember which one was the Lady. For clarity, the gimmicked corner is now blue in our example. The spectator will, of course, choose the middle card.

8

Slowly slide out the bottom card and place it face down on top of the other two. Repeat this with the original middle card (now marked with an X in our example).

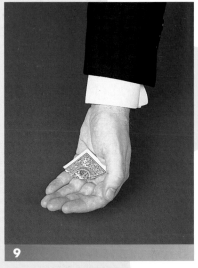

9

As you slide this card out and place it on the top, the gimmicked pocket will dislodge and drop into your hand, where the three cards will provide ample cover.

The dANGERS OF impressiNG YOUR AUdieNCe too mUch Any magician will tell you that audiences sometimes react to a magic effect in ways that are totally unexpected. However, few modern day performers face the open hostility with which their forebears had to contend on a daily basis. In 15th century Cologne, for example, a girl found herself charged with witchcraft when, in the presence of spectators, she tore a handkerchief into pieces and 'immediately afterwards produced it whole'. A juggler who, in 1571, had entertained several audiences with simple card tricks in Paris, found himself imprisoned for life on a similar charge. A performer named Triscalinus, performing before Charles IX of France caused the rings to fly from the fingers of a bemused courtier onto his own. No sooner had he performed the feat than 'the company rose against him and forced him to confess satanic aid'!

As you do so, it becomes clear why it's useful to use two corresponding cards. If the first card turned over is widely different from any in the original fan, your spectator's suspicions will be aroused. However, since you did not draw attention to any card other than the Queen, your audience is unlikely to notice that the three of Hearts has mysteriously appeared.

You can now spread the cards out in front of you and challenge your spectator to 'Find the Lady' and to offer a wager, if you wish.

Fan the three cards face down. As you do, say 'I feel like a wager', and, with your left hand, reach into your pocket to acquire your 'stake money'. In reality, this gives you an opportunity to ditch the gimmick.

If you are so inclined you have the opportunity to wager twice more before revealing that the Queen has, infact, vanished.

SAWING a LAdy IN HAlF

One of magic's best-known illusions is that of sawing a lady in half. In this version of the classic trick you are going to cut a Queen in half and then, miraculously, restore her. Properly presented this miniature version can be a real audience baffler and enhance your reputation as a wonder worker no end!

YOU WILL NEED
A manila wage envelope
A Queen playing card
A pair of scissors.

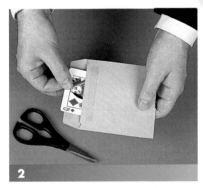

Announce that you are about to perform one of magic's best-known illusions and introduce your 'beautiful assistant'. Push the Queen into the envelope, with the slit turned away from your audience.

As you do so, ensure that the card exits via the slit. Practise doing this until you can do it smoothly and confidently. Any hesitation at this point will alert the audience to the trickery.

You will first need to prepare the envelope by cutting a slit, through which the Queen (of Diamonds in our example) can easily fit.

5

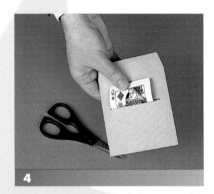

4

As the card slides out, grip its upper edge and bend it back against the upper half of the envelope, towards the flap. Again, practise this until you can execute the necessary moves smoothly and confidently. Remember that the envelope provides sufficient cover to hide the true trickery from your audience.

The audience's view and therefore their perception is that the Queen has gone all the way into the envelope. You can even leave the upper portion of her face peeking out. With the scissors, cut the envelope in half, apparently cutting the Queen in two. She, of course, is safely bent back against the upper section of the envelope. Be sure to cut along the slit that you created, in order to destroy the evidence of how the illusion was achieved.

fANCY ThAt! The 'sawing' illusion was invented by P.T. Selbit (1879–1938). In his version, which he called 'sawing through a woman', his volunteer was tied with ropes inside a large box. A saw was then passed through both her and the box without harming her. This technique was improved by Polish-American magician Horace Goldin (1874–1939), who gave it a sensational twist. In his version the box was separated, giving the impression that the woman had indeed been sawn in half. A talented self-publicist, Goldin would advertize in the local press for girls willing to be sawn in half, guaranteeing them '$10,000 in cases of fatality'! Ambulances would be parked outside the theatre, top-hatted undertakers paraded up and down the Street, while nurses with stretchers would stand around in the lobby as the audience arrived.

6

Separate the two halves of the envelope for a few moments, allowing the situation to register with the audience.

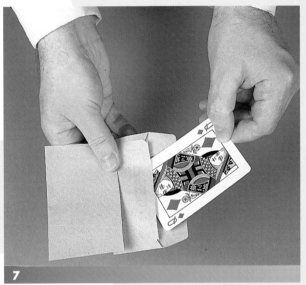

7

Touching the halves back together and clipping them with your right thumb, release your grip on the bend, take the upper section of the card in your left hand, and pull the fully restored Queen out of the envelope.

afterthought You will need to be familiar with exactly how a card bends. Too much pressure can result in a suspicious crease appearing on the restored Queen. Alternatively you can perform the illusion with a borrowed note or bill, a picture from a magazine or even a photograph of someone you know.

The cut and restored rope

In *The Discoverie Of Witchcraft*, Reginald Scott reveals the secret of how 'you may seeme to cut asunder any lace and, with witchcraft or conjuration to make it closed together againe'. The same trick is still being performed by magicians the world over under the simpler title of 'The Cut and Restored Rope'.

YOU WILL NEED

A length of rope

A piece of the same rope approximately 25 cm (10 inches) long

A pair of scissors.

Approach your audience holding the longer rope in your right hand, with the smaller one looped and hidden in your left hand. Have them inspect the longer piece. (For purposes of clarification our example shows two different coloured ropes).

Explain that you are about to perform one of the oldest magic tricks known to man and, folding the longer rope in half, casually place its looped centre into your left hand, so that it almost covers the hidden loop. Close your fist around it.

5

Taking your scissors, cut through this gimmick loop. As your audience sees it, you have cut one long piece of rope into two.

4

The reality is, of course, that you are infact holding two pieces of rope in your hand, with your clenched fist concealing what you don't want your audience to see.

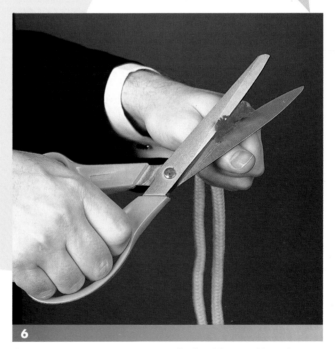

6

Snip away at the shorter rope until all evidence of its existence lies in tiny pieces on the floor. Take extra care, since you will be cutting close to your fingers.

Using your favourite magic words, blow onto your clenched fist and crack the rope, as though it were a whip, giving the impression that this is the magic moment when you have 'made it closed againe'.

BANgle on rope

In this simple routine you allow a spectator to tie your wrists together. You then introduce a bangle, which you allow the audience to examine to ensure that it contains no breaks or gaps. Retrieving the bangle, you turn your back for a moment, then turn around to show that the bangle is now threaded onto the rope, even though the knots are still securely fastened around your wrists.

YOU WILL NEED

A length of soft rope

Two identical bangles.

1

Out of sight of your audience, push one of the bangles over your hand and hide it up your sleeve.

2

Approach a spectator holding the rope and the other bangle and invite them to tie you up.

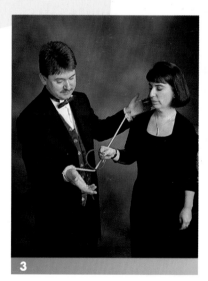

3

Ask the spectator to inspect the bangle, then to press it against the rope until they are satisfied that the bangle cannot pass through or onto the rope.

4

Turning your back on the audience, dispose of the bangle by slipping it into a convenient pocket.

5

At the same time, allow the duplicate to slip from your sleeve, over your hand and onto the rope.

6

Face the spectator showing that you have, somehow, managed to cause the rope and bangle to become linked.

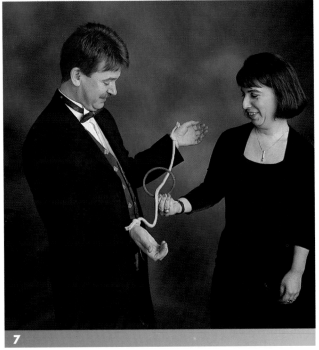

7

The audience can examine everything, since no evidence remains as to how you accomplished this 'miracle'.

It's knot ON

The routine that follows is a very strong, visual piece of magic that's not a bad trick, either. In front of a spectator you tie a knot in a piece of rope, then remove the knot and hand it to your spectator as a souvenir. Such a souvenir will enable them to show evidence of your skills to their friends.

YOU WILL NEED

A length of soft rope

A gimmick knot, for which you will
    need a pair of scissors.

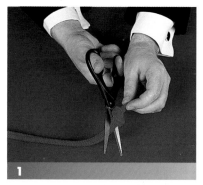

1

To create the gimmick knot, simply tie a knot in the rope you intend to use for the routine and cut it off this section. If you intend to use this gimmick more than once, it is as well to dab its ends with a little glue to prevent fraying.

With the gimmicked knot concealed in the curled fingers of your left hand, approach your spectator and hand them the long rope. Ask them to inspect it and, when they have done so, tell them that you are puzzled by a strange power that you seem to have developed.

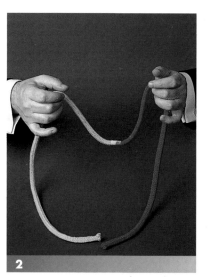

2

Take back the rope and hold it so that the centre sags into a U-bend. For clarification purposes we have coloured the two halves of the rope yellow and red. Follow these step-by-step instructions very closely. Don't worry if the trick doesn't work the first time, keep at it and the necessary moves will suddenly come together.

3

Make a loop with the rope, bringing the right side up behind the left side.

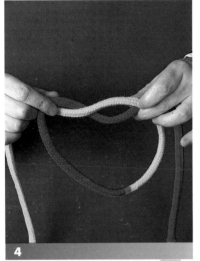

Clip the points where the two cross between your thumbs and forefingers.

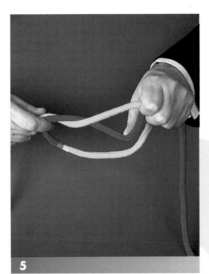

Push the rope down with your left thumb into the lower section of the loop.

As you do so, begin pulling on the right side so that the rope fastens around your thumb.

As the rope pulls tighter, remove your thumb from the loop allowing the rope to form a knot. Practise these moves until you can tie the knot quickly and confidently.

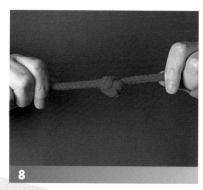

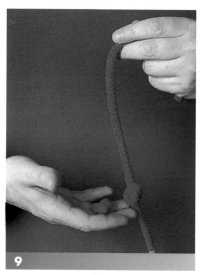

With practice you will be able to pull on the rope until the knot appears to be firm. However, if you tug sharply on the ends of the rope, the knot will disappear. We have now changed the rope to just one colour to emphasise the knot.

Once the knot is tied, curl your left fingers around it (that are also hiding the gimmick knot) and grip it tightly.

Pulling the rope through your fist, act as though you are trying to pull the knot off the rope.

When you feel the moment is right, let go of the rope, show the gimmick knot and give it to your spectator as a souvenir.

The *rope* Through BODY Illusion

In this final piece of 'Clever Stuff', you cause a spectator to apparently pull two pieces of rope straight through your body. Its success depends largely on your ability to hide the crucial moves from the audience. Since this illusion is dependent on swift and fluid moves you will need to practise until you are fluent with the necessary stages involved.

YOU WILL NEED

Two pieces of rope approximately
2 metres (6 foot) long
A small piece of cotton thread.

First, fold both pieces of rope in half and tie the middles together with the thread. In our sequence of photographs we have used different coloured ropes and bound the centres with black tape for clarity and emphasis. Obviously when you come to perform the routine, the ropes should be the same colour and the thread virtually invisible.

Approach your spectator with the two lengths of rope draped over your outstretched hand, your thumb concealing the thread that binds them together.

Facing your audience, take the two lengths of rope over your head so that the same piece of rope is hanging over each shoulder. The different coloured ropes in our picture demonstrate what you should have done.

4

Tuck the centres into your collar.

5

Pull the ropes around your neck asking the spectator to thread them down your sleeves. As the audience sees it, you now have two pieces of rope wrapped around your body.

6

Once the ropes have been threaded down both sleeves, ask your spectator to pick up one rope from each sleeve and tie the ends together.

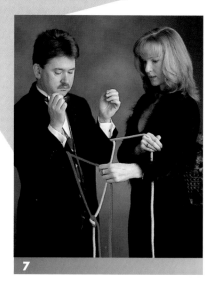

7

This done, ask them to pick up the other two ends and give them a sharp tug. In the pictures we have tied a double knot for purposes of clarification. In practice the ropes should be tied overhand once only without creating a knot.

8

By tugging on the ropes the spectator will snap the thread, causing the two ropes to separate and pull out of your sleeves. To the audience it will appear that the ropes have actually passed through your body.

5

NUMEROLOGICAL miRACLes

Numbers have always been considered magical. In this chapter you will learn how to use them in all manner of strange and bizarre routines, from predicting what number a spectator will think of to revealing the correct hour of their birth. Virtually all the effects are very simple, but with the right presentation, can create some of the most astonishing routines.

The eternal eights

Anyone who could truly predict the future would become an instant celebrity. With this neat little routine you may not find worldwide fame, but you'll be able to impress your friends and workmates and, with the right presentation, gain a reputation as a soothsayer! Work hard at creating an air of mystery around the effect, so that you give a credible performance.

YOU WILL NEED

A deck of cards

An envelope containing your

prediction.

1

Arrange three piles of cards face down upon the table. The first pile should consist of the four Eights. The value of the cards in the second pile should total eight. The third pile should consist of eight cards.

You do not want to present this routine as a magic trick but rather an 'experiment in prediction', so it is a good idea to bring out the whole deck to begin with, albeit prearranged. Arrange the cards that total eight on top of the deck, remembering how many of them there are. The four Eights you can remove, one by one, as you act mysterious and look through the deck to 'get an impression of the future'. The eight cards? Just look at the backs of the cards as though trying to 'pick up a vibe', but without drawing attention to the exact number. Be as dramatic as you wish because presentation is everything.

On a piece of paper write, 'It is my prediction that you will find the eternal eight pile,' and hand it to your spectator. Now ask them to select any of the piles.

Whichever pile they select, your prediction is correct! To add to the air of mystery you may like to know that for numerological purposes, eight symbolizes fullness; and, when laid horizontally, the figure 8 is the symbol of infinity.

numeROlogy

n this impressive routine you demonstrate the principles of numerology to your audience. Writing a prediction upon a piece of paper, you place it in full view and then ask a spectator to choose a number. Counting out the corresponding number of cards, you ask a member of your audience to read out your prediction and they find that you have correctly predicted the card that their number would lead to.

YOU WILL NEED

A deck of cards

A piece of paper on which you write
your prediction.

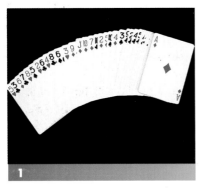

Locate the tenth card in the deck (in our example it is the Eight of Clubs), and remember it. Look into your spectator's eyes as though studying their innermost thoughts and write the name of the tenth card on a piece of paper.

Fold your prediction, set it down in full view of the audience and explain that you wish to try an experiment in numerology. Ask your subject to name any number between 10 and 20. In our example the number 12 has been chosen.

Whatever their choice, count that number of cards face down onto the table. We have placed an X on the Eight of Clubs to help you keep track of it and to help you understand the mechanics of the trick.

Explain that according to numerologists, you can tell much about a person by studying numbers that are relevant to them. However those numbers must first be added together to create a single figure. So in the case of 12 it is 1 + 2, giving 3.

As you say this, count two cards face down, pause at the third card and say, 'So according to the laws of numerology, a number that you freely selected has brought you to this card.' Turn the card face up, revealing its identity.

Point out that your prediction has been in view at all times and let them read it. They will be amazed to find the name of the card that 'they' selected.

where in the world

This is an easy to do card trick dressed up as a numerogical miracle that dangles the possibility of the chance for an exotic holiday at your expense before a spectator. Having enticed the spectator with the promise of a trip to a far away destination, they discover that they are, infact, going nowhere!

YOU WILL NEED

Approximately 36 blank cards

A pen.

● Out of sight of your audience write the names of desirable holiday destinations on thirty-five of the blank cards. On the remaining card write 'NOWHERE' and arrange the stack of place names so that the 'NOWHERE' card is tenth from the top.

● Inform your spectator that you are feeling in a particularly generous mood and that you would like to pay for them to enjoy a holiday at your expense in any one of these exotic locations. As you say this casually run through the cards showing the different destinations but being careful not to alter the sequence or flash the 'Nowhere' card.

● Tell them that, unfortunately, since it will be a last minute booking it will have to be with one of those airlines that stop everywhere. Hand them the cards and say, 'Please count from the top the number of stopovers you wish to make. Keep in mind they will affect your journey time, so suggest you choose no more than ten.'

● Turn away as they do the count and ask them to hide the stopovers so you can have no idea of the number chosen.

● When they have finished counting, take back the cards and say, 'Now let's plan your flight path.' As you say this begin counting cards face down in a line on the table from right to left.

● Without drawing attention to the fact count out exactly ten cards and, turning to your audience say, 'Well there you have a nice selection of holiday destinations; are you ready to fly?' If they say 'yes' ask, 'So tell me, how many stopovers did you choose to make?'

● Whatever their answer, beginning with the far left card turn over that number of cards. So, for example, if they chose three stopovers you would turn over three cards. The next card along will be the 'Nowhere' card that was tenth from the top.

● Turn to your spectator and continue, 'Well, those are the destinations you chose not to stay at and this is the destination that I am going send you to at my own expense.' Slowly turn that card over and reveal that they are going 'NOWHERE'.

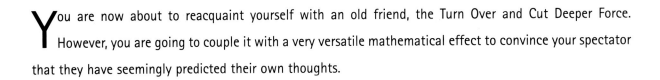

ThE MYStiCА1 numbeR

You are now about to reacquaint yourself with an old friend, the Turn Over and Cut Deeper Force. However, you are going to couple it with a very versatile mathematical effect to convince your spectator that they have seemingly predicted their own thoughts.

YOU WILL NEED

A deck of cards.

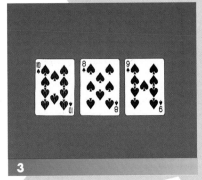

2

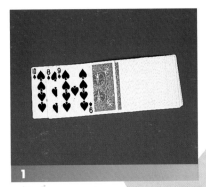

1

Place a Ten, Eight and Nine of any suit on top of the deck. Our example uses the Spades.

3

Ask your spectator to perform the Turn Over and Cut Deeper (see page 26) force until all three cards have been placed down on the table.

Hand them a piece of paper on which to write any three-digit number between 100 and 1,000. They must then reverse this number and subtract the lower figure from the higher. Let's say the spectator chooses 568.

568

865

865 – 568 = 297

Having reached a total that you stress could not have been known to anybody, say you wish to remove any chance from the equation. Ask them to reverse their total and add those two numbers together.

297

792

297 + 792 = 1089

Tell the spectator not to show you their final total, but first to turn over their 'freely chosen' cards. This will reveal a Ten, an Eight and a Nine. Now look at their total, and, if they haven't already noticed and fallen to the ground in supplication before you, point out that their choice of cards predicted the total before they even chose a number.

If you follow the instructions exactly as written, it doesn't matter what number they choose – the total will always be 1089. This is just one way of presenting the mystery. Use your imagination to devise others and see where it leads you.

BOOKWORM

Some seemingly impossible routines in mental magic involve using a spectator's personal information – birthdays, anniversaries and so on. This magnificent routine enables you to predict the exact word in a book that corresponds with a stranger's important anniversaries.

YOU WILL NEED
A pen and paper
A book or local phone directory.

The information required from your volunteer is as follows:
(the information given is based upon this book's year of publication, 2001).

The year of your birth	1968
Your age at the end of this year	33
The year you began your present career	1985
The number of years in your chosen career	16
TOTAL	4002

This is a fictitious example and everyone's information will, of course, be different. But what everyone will share in common is that, if you add the dates and years together, the total will always be twice the current year, in this example, 4002. Try it with your own information.

You can use any combination of anniversaries, such as the number of years a spectator has been married, the years that children were born and so on. As long as the questions are laid out exactly as above, the result will always be the same.

● You could have the spectator break the total down. For example you could ask them to take the first two digits of their number and open the local phone book at that page – page 40. With the last two digits they count that number of lines down the left column – 02 – and concentrate on that name and number. You will, of course, have already looked them up and noted them. As they concentrate, pretend to write something onto a piece of paper. Hand it to them and let them see that you were apparently able to read their mind.

● You could look up the first word on line 2 of page 40 of any book and reveal it.

● You could even memorize line 2 on page 40 and give the spectator a visual interpretation of what they are reading. So, for example, if it describes someone standing by a fire say, 'I'm beginning to feel a warm glow... as though there is heat somewhere.'

As with so many of these mystical routines you are limited only by your own imagination. But you now have at your disposal a tried and tested principle that really will pack a hefty punch.

WHAT'S IN A NAME? HOCUS POCUS In the 16th century, hocus pocus was generally used to describe both a magician and his tricks. There are several explanations for its origins. Many of the clergy in Europe, ever vigilant for acts of profanity from those they suspected of being in league with the Devil, accused magicians of corrupting the Latin used at the most solemn moments of the mass – *Hoc est enim Corpus meum*. Others thought its origins were Italian wonder workers, who entreated the long dead wizard Ochus Bochus to assist them in their conjuring. Whichever is true, the term was being used extensively by the early 17th century, with a leading performer of the time even billing himself 'The King's Majesty's most excellent Hocus Pocus.' The word hoax probably began as a shortened version of hocus.

The eyes HAVe It

Numbers can be used to perform many varied and impressive magical routines. With a little imagination you can turn an equation into a baffling mystery. In this next bit of clever jiggery-pokery. You apparently discover the random results of a spectator's actions by reading the pupils of their eyes!

YOU WILL NEED

20 golf balls or other fairly large round objects

A bag.

1

Show your audience what appears to be a random number of golf balls, tip them into a bag and ask for a volunteer.

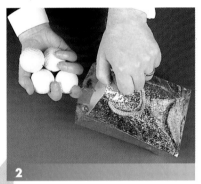

2

Hold out the bag, turning your head away, and ask the spectator to reach inside it and remove a random number of golf balls. The reason I always perform this routine with golf balls is that it is imperative that no more than 10 are removed. No matter how big their hands, most people would find it difficult to grasp more than this. In our example, 4 have been taken out.

3

Keeping your head turned, ask the spectator to discard those golf balls, empty the bag and count how many remain. If a single number remains, the spectator must remove that number and discard them. If the number remaining has two digits, they must add these two numbers together and discard the total. In our example, 16 remain.

$$1 + 6 = 7$$

So 7 golf balls would be discarded.

4

The spectator must now count the number that remain and concentrate on them. After a few moments ask them to come and stand in front of you. Look deep into their eyes and say that it was once believed you could see a likeness of the last thing a person saw imprinted upon their pupils. Explain that you have discovered that this actually works, and say, 'I see that you last looked at 9 golf balls... Is that correct?'

Because you started with 20 balls and the number your spectator could grasp, the final number will always be 9. You have shown your mystical powers literally 'in the eyes of your audience'.

TO BE OR NOT TO BE – The elephants in Denmark

This routine with its kicker ending, is one of my favourites. It works just as effectively with 100 people as it does with 1 and often draws gasps of amazement from several members of the audience. To show you how it works I'll just do it on you here and now. Are you sitting comfortably? Then I'll begin!

Think of a number between 1 and 10. Got one? Good. Now double it.
Add 8 to this new total. Take your time!
Divide this new total by 2. You're doing very well.
Subtract the original number you thought of from this final total.
Whatever your final number is, match it to a letter of the alphabet. So 1 = A , 2= B, 3 = C and so on.
Now think of a country that begins with that letter, anywhere in the world.
Look at the second letter of that country's name and think of an animal that begins with that letter.
Concentrate on the animal's colour. A little harder please.
That can't be...! There are no grey elephants in Denmark.
Did I guess right? The fact is that all numbers between 1 and 10, when added and subtracted like that, will always result in half the total of the second number added, in this case 8. Had I asked you to add 12 to your number the final answer would have been 6.

The number 4 corresponds with the letter D and most people will think of Denmark and then an elephant. This can occasionally backfire when someone thinks of Djibouti or the Dominican Republic, or if they think of an echidna or even an eagle or emu, but if you perform it for a larger group, the fact that some audience members think of a different animal, will enhance your reputation since it shows that they could have had another choice.

WHAT'S IN A NAME? WAND The magic wand is a symbol of the magician's mystical powers. Perhaps the most famous example of wands being used for supernatural purposes were the rods of Moses and Aaron which were used to part the waters of the Red Sea, to cause water to gush from a rock in the desert, and to confound the enchantments of Pharaoh's magicians.

The modern conjuror's wand can be traced back to the magicians' wands of the Middle Ages that were used in various magical rites, including attempts to communicate with Satan! In modern magic, a wand is an excellent tool for misdirection. Reaching into a pocket to remove it can provide the cover for ditching a gimmick. Using it to gesture can be used to make an audience look away from where the trickery is taking place. Holding it in your hand can provide a valid excuse for keeping your fist closed when you are hiding something in it.

The word is evolved from the Norse word *vondr* meaning 'thin straight stick'.

and The HOUR OF YOUR BiRth WAS...

The psychic miracle that follows will either convince people that you can truly read their minds, or that you have friends in high places with access to personal information! You will seemingly reveal the hour at which the spectator was born. And leave them worrying what else you know about them!

YOU WILL NEED

A deck of cards, one of which will be secretly marked

A pen

A piece of paper.

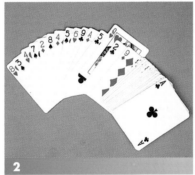

To begin with, you need to secretly mark a card so that you will be able to identify it later. In the example we will be using the Queen of Hearts, so with a sharp knife we have put a tiny scrape on two opposite corners. In the picture, these marks are on the top left-hand and bottom right-hand corners.

Place the card thirteenth in the deck, and you are ready to perform.

Find a spectator who knows the hour of their birth and ask them to concentrate on it in their mind's eye. Stress that they must use the 12-hour clock and tell them not to bother with the minutes, just the hour.

Stare for a few moments, as though trying to discern what they are thinking, then write QUEEN OF HEARTS on a piece of paper, fold it and set it down on the table. Say, 'This is the image I located in your mind's eye. I can't change what is written, and it will now stay in view at all times.'

Hand the cards to your spectator. Ask them to count, from the top, the number of cards that correspond to the hour of their birth, and place them out of sight. Turn away as they do this. In our example the spectator counts eight cards. And stress that you will not look until the spectator tells you that they have done as you asked.

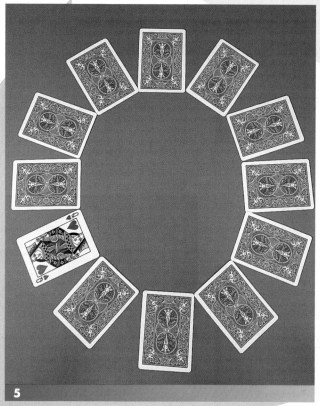

5

4

Once the cards have been hidden, turn back and retrieve the deck. Tell your spectator that you are going to create their birth clock and, beginning with the 12, lay out a counter-clockwise circle. As you do this, look for the location of the marked card, which is at 8 o'clock. You now know the hour of the spectator's birth.

Look at your spectator and say, 'Have we ever met?' When they confirm that you are strangers, ask nonchalantly, 'So is there any way I could know that you were born at 8 o'clock?' Just watch as their jaw hits the floor. Then get them to confirm that they were, indeed, born at 8 o'clock.

Ask the spectator to turn over the card at 8 o'clock, revealing, in the example, that it is the Queen of Hearts. Ask, 'Do you remember that when you were merely thinking of the hour, I wrote a prediction on that slip of paper?' Give them time to agree, then ask them to read the prediction aloud.

PSYChiC OR MAGiCiAN?

The final numerological effect couples the Turn Over and Cut Deeper force with a standard magical routine known as 'spelling the card'. You first show how a magician would perform a card trick – by allowing the spectator to choose a card then revealing its identity. Next you show that a psychic would, of course, know in advance which card the spectator would choose.

YOU WILL NEED

A specially-prepared deck of cards.

1

Whereas with the majority of routines in this book I have encouraged you to make your own choices, I suggest that in this effect you follow my example to the letter. Set the Eight of Spades to one side. Remove and arrange in this order the Ten of Clubs, Six of Hearts, Nine of Spades, Three of Hearts, Jack of Diamonds and Seven of Diamonds.

2

To help identify their locations, we have placed an X on their reverse sides. I suggest you place a very light pencil dot on the back of the Ten of Clubs and Seven of Diamonds to help you locate them later. Place them on the deck and put nine indifferent cards on top of them.

3

Put the Eight of Spades on top and you're ready to perform.

Say to your audience, 'People often ask me how to tell the difference between a magician and a psychic. It is a question to which I have devoted years of study and I think I now have the answer, which I shall demonstrate with this deck of cards'. As you do so, fan the cards in front of a spectator to show that 'all the cards are different'.

4

Setting the cards down, have your spectator perform the Turn Over and Cut Deeper force (see page 26) and take the first face-down card they have cut to. When they have done so, say, 'A magician would tell you that you have picked the Eight of Spades.' Have the spectator show the card to confirm that this is indeed the case.

5

As the spectator does this, casually pick up the deck and transfer all the face up cards to the bottom of the deck, turning them face down as you do so.

6

Spread the cards out with the faces towards the spectator. Practise doing this so that you can easily locate the pencil dots on the reverse of the Ten of Clubs and Seven of Diamonds and so that you are able to spread them in such away that the audience only sees these and the four cards between. Ensure that the spectator only gets a brief glimpse as you ask them to remember any card.

7

Closing the fan, place the cards on the table and ask the spectator what card they are thinking of. Whatever their selection, say, 'A psychic would have known beforehand that you would choose that card.' In our example, the spectator chooses the Jack of Diamonds. So begin to lay the cards out in a row on the table, beginning with the top card, giving a letter to each as you spell out J-A-C-K O-F D-I-A-M-O-N-D. Then pause dramatically and say triumphantly, 'S'. Turning over the final card, reveal it to be the Jack of Diamonds. Smile and say, 'So I guess that makes me a psychic magician.'

6

esp, psychic & spooky magic

The art of supposedly seeing the future or communing with the spirits is as old as mankind itself. Today, creating effects such as these is known as bizarre magic and, although sometimes frowned upon by purists, its effect on an audience is the closest you will ever come to being perceived as having done real magic.

an esp experiment

ESP (extrasensory perception) and mind reading hold a fascination for many people, and in the following 'test' you will demonstrate your ability to influence another person's actions with the power of your mind. This simple effect will leave your audience both astonished and baffled.

YOU WILL NEED
3 ESP cards comprising:
The star
The square
The wavy lines
A pen
A card box or envelope
Paper.

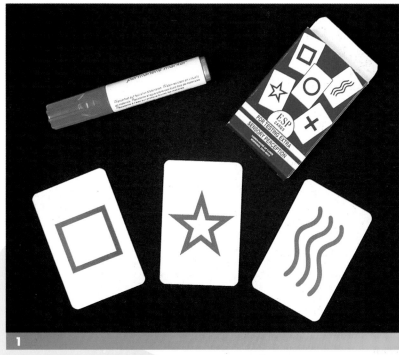

Either buy a set of ESP cards, or scrawl the necessary symbols onto three pieces of blank card. On the back of the star, write in bold black letters YOU WILL CHOOSE THIS CARD. Place all three cards into the card box or envelope. On a blank piece of card write STOP AT THE WAVY LINES and place this inside the card box or envelope as well. On a small piece of paper write STOP AT THE SQUARE. Fold it, tuck it into the cap of the pen, recap the pen and you are ready to perform.

Tell your audience that you are about to demonstrate your ability to influence people's actions using nothing more than the power of your mind. Ask for a volunteer.

Take out the box (or envelope) containing your ESP cards and, being careful not to expose the writing on the back of the star, lay them out in front of your audience with the star in the middle. Casually drop the box next to them. Take out the pen and hand it to your volunteer.

Ask them to wave the pen over the cards and place it upon the symbol that most appeals to them.

Most people choose the star because a) it's in the middle and b) it is the most striking of the symbols. If they do, say, 'You had a free choice. Do you agree?' They will nod. Shake your head and ask them to turn over the card and read out what it says on the back. Of course, it says YOU WILL CHOOSE THIS CARD. Alarmed, they will turn over the others to find the backs blank.

If they choose the wavy lines, ask them to open the box and remove the ONLY card in there. If they choose the square, just ask them to uncap the pen, take out the piece of paper and read what it says.

The PSYCHIC GRApe

There are occasions when a fact of science can be hijacked by a magician who, using nothing more than a little acting, turns the natural into the supernatural. This effect does just that. Tell your audience that you wish to demonstrate your abilities of psychokinesis, the ability to make inanimate objects move with your mind.

YOU WILL NEED

A glass of carbonated drink

A grape.

1

Drop the grape into the glass and allow it to sink to the bottom.

2

Gently stroke the rim of the glass and pretend to expound an incredible amount of mental energy.

3

After a few moments of this apparent coaxing, the grape will begin to move slowly and then, to your audience's amazement, will rise to the top of the glass. When it does, watch it very carefully. Sometimes it will float on top of the liquid, in which case end the trick. At other times you will see it begin to sink again. If it does, the moment you notice it happening, take your finger away from the glass and let your audience see that the grape sinks without your assistance! At this point, hand the grape to a spectator asking them to confirm it is an ordinary grape. As they inspect it, drink the liquid, thus destroying any clue as to how the miracle occurred.

COLOUR SENSOR

This is a simple routine to perform but, presented with confidence, it will leave your audience clueless as to how you are able to identify a colour by touch alone. Tell your audience that you have been studying the art of colour divination, and have discovered that you possess the ability to sense a colour simply by feeling it.

YOU WILL NEED

Several different coloured wax crayons (I always use three).

Hand the coloured crayons to a spectator, turn away and place your hands behind your back. Ask that they place any colour into your hand. When they have done so, ask them to hide the other crayons.

Turn to face your audience, keeping your hands behind your back, but as you do so scrape a fingernail along the crayon. This will leave a deposit of the wax behind your nail.

Keeping the crayon behind your back, gesture at your audience with the other hand, showing your open palm. This will demonstrate that you have no paper hidden there, and that you haven't drawn onto your hand – the theories that an audience often comes up with. Oddly, no one ever thinks to check your fingernails!

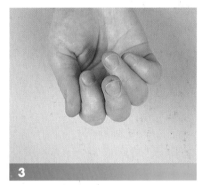

Assume your pose of mystical concentration and bring your clenched hand to your forehead as though to aid your thoughts. As you do so, you will clearly see the minute deposit of wax behind your fingernail. You can then reveal the colour of the crayon.

GRAphology

Explain to your audience that you have been researching the art of graphology, which means deciphering personality traits from a person's handwriting. To demonstrate, you ask three volunteers to provide examples of their handwriting while your back is turned. Another spectator hands them to you and you proceed to identify one spectator's handwriting.

YOU WILL NEED

A piece of paper

A pen.

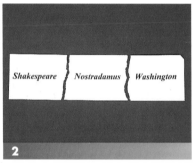

As you will see from the picture, when you tear the paper into three, the two outer pieces have one jagged edge each, while the centre piece has two jagged edges, enabling easy identification.

Standing before the spectators, talk a little about how it is possible to tell a great deal about someone by studying their handwriting. As you do this, casually tear the paper into three equal pieces and hand them out, noting which spectator receives the centre piece.

Ask them to write down a line of poetry or a name. Here, the name NOSTRADAMUS has the two jagged edges, so this is the one we will be working with.

Ask your spectators to fold their papers in half and half again, place them on the table and jumble them up. Turning round you will be able to see which of the three was the centre piece because it will be the only one with two jagged edges. If you were to pick that up straight away and identify the handwriting, your audience might become suspicious. So we return to the Magician's Choice (see page 30).

Ask a spectator to pick up two of the papers. If they select the two original outer edges say, 'Fine. I shall work with this one', and pick the one left behind.

If they choose an outer piece and the original centre piece, ask them to hand one of them to you. If they hand you the centre piece, open it and begin your reading. If they retain the centre piece, say, 'So that is your choice. Please hand it to me.'

Study the writing and then begin to describe the impressions you are receiving. Describe the hair and eye colour of the person who wrote it. If you know their job, describe the sort of things they do. If you know their hobbies explain a little about those. Finally, turn to the person and say, 'I believe it was you who wrote this.'

now you see it

In the following routine you appear to cause a card that a spectator is merely thinking of to disappear. Properly performed this effect can draw gasps of amazement from an audience. Of course the actual magic is more to do with what the spectators think they see as opposed to what they actually see!

YOU WILL NEED
12 playing cards
1 Joker
A pair of scissors
Glue.

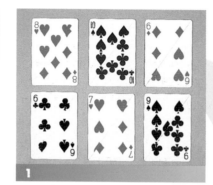

The six gimmicked cards are actually twelve cards cut in half and glued together. Study the picture on the left carefully. You will see that the first card, the Eight of Hearts, has the Eight of Diamonds as its lower half. Look at each card in the picture to see how they are constructed.

Place the Joker at the face of the packet and approach your spectator.

Tell your spectator that you want them to look briefly at some cards and remember one of them. Fan the cards and hold them up in front of your spectator saying, 'Don't pick the Joker, that's too easy.' Close the fan and ask the spectator to concentrate on the card they chose in their mind's eye. As they do so, casually turn the deck over.

Announce that you will attempt to make their card vanish from the packet. Fan the cards and ask, 'Has the card you were thinking of disappeared?'

It certainly has, and your audience will, hopefully, be suitably astonished. Of course, all the original cards have disappeared. But, thanks to the similarity of the values, the brief glimpse you allowed your spectator and the fact you asked them to focus on just one card means they will only notice that their card has vanished.

you DO VOODOO

This effect is actually very simple to perform. However that doesn't mean it is easy. You will need to be both confident and nonchalant in the way you literally handle your spectator if you are to be successful. That said, it is a very effective and astonishing routine and will leave your spectator totally baffled.

YOU WILL NEED

A small amount of ash or crushed charcoal.

When no one's looking, moisten the tips of your index fingers and give them a liberal dusting of ash from an ashtray.

Approach your victim (sorry, spectator) and ask, 'Can I just ask you to do something for me?' As you do, take them by the hands and pull them towards you. In so doing, you will transfer the ash from your fingertips onto the palms of their hands. Don't make a big thing of it, just do it and then let go instantly. You do not want them to remember that you touched them.

Ask this person to clench their fists and extend their arms. Explain that you are a practitioner of the ancient art of sympathetic magic, which today is more commonly known as voodoo. Start moving your hands around and ask them to do likewise. It is important that you put time between placing the ash and revealing that they have ash in their hands.

fANCY ThAt! OOPS! In 1977 the hypnotist Romark announced that he was going to demonstrate his psychic powers by driving a car, blindfold, through Ilford in Essex, England. On October 12th, suitably blinded, he took his seat behind the wheel of his Renault, nudged the accelerator and set off, with only his psychic vision to guide him. His audience watched in astonishment as he promptly drove into the back of a parked police van. 'It was parked where logic told me it wouldn't be' he later told admiring spectators!

Smear two little circles of ash on the back of your spectator's hands, slowly rubbing it with your fingers, humming a mystical note as you do so.

Dip your fingers into the ashtray so that you have plenty of ash on them once more.

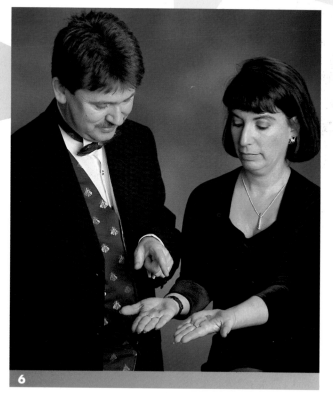

Dust off the ash and ask, 'Did you feel the power of voodoo at work?' When they shake their head say, 'Then turn over your hands and open them.' Just watch their face when they see that the ash has mysteriously reappeared on their palms.

fORetelliNg The fUtURe

In this clever routine you attempt to convince your spectator that you possess the gift of seeing the future. To demonstrate it, you correctly predict, under seemingly impossible conditions, exactly which card they will choose.

YOU WILL NEED

A deck of cards.

Inform your audience that you are a trainee psychic, able to predict things that will happen within the next ten minutes or so. To demonstrate this impressive skill, ask a volunteer to give the deck of cards a thorough shuffle.

1

Once this is done, stress that you do not want to touch the cards. Ask your spectator to fan them out and hold them with the faces pointing towards you. Concentrate a little, then say, 'I think I know exactly which of these cards you are going to choose.'

2

Have the cards passed in front of you in such a way that you, but not the spectator, can see the faces. You must remember the first and second cards of the deck, in our example the Three of Clubs and the Jack of Hearts.

3

Later in the trick you will use the top card to denote the suit of the chosen card (Clubs) and the second to denote its value (Jack). So as the spectator waves the cards to and fro, look for the Jack of Clubs. When you see it say, 'Wait, there's the card I've seen you choose.' Reach across and, without letting anyone else see it, remove the card and place it face down on the table.

Stress that you have made your decision, you have placed a prediction on the table and you cannot change your mind.

Ask them to pick up their dealt pile and deal it into two piles. The last card dealt will be the original top card. The top card on the other pile will be the original second card.

Ask your spectator to begin dealing cards face down onto the table and to stop wherever they choose. When they stop, the original first and second card from the top will now be the bottom two of the dealt pile.

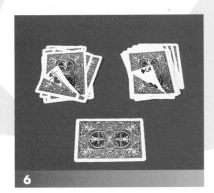

Ask the spectator to point to one of the two piles. If they point to the pile with the suit card on top say, 'So this pile will denote the suit.' Turn it over to reveal the suit, in our example Clubs. Point to the other pile and say, 'This will denote the value of the card.' Turn the card over to reveal, in our example, the Jack.

It is time now to reiterate just how random the procedure has been. Say, 'Let's just recap. You shuffled the cards. I haven't touched them other than to select my prediction, which has been in full view at all times. You counted the cards, stopping wherever you chose. The card that you appear to have chosen is the Jack of Clubs.' At this point turn over your prediction card and reveal that you were indeed able to see into the future.

coincimentAl

With this intriguing routine you talk to your audience about coincidences and say a strange thing you have recently discovered puzzles you. Offering to demonstrate it you have a spectator mark an X on the *back* of any card and lose it in the deck. You then have them place an X on the *face* of a card. When this card is turned over it is found to have an X on its reverse side.

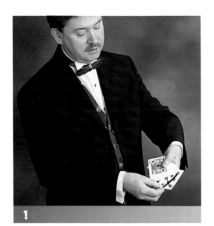

Out of your audience's sight put an X on the front and back of a card in the deck. Later on it must look like the Xs were scrawled by the spectator behind their back, so mark this card behind your back. Slip the card into the centre of the deck and approach your spectator.

When they fail to find a card with an X on the back say, 'I wonder where it could be'. As you do so turn over the marked card and reveal that the spectator has put an X on the front and back of the same card. 'Now that's a coincidence'.

Ask if your spectator believes in coincidence. If they reply yes say 'what a coincidence, so do I'. If their answer is negative say 'what a coincidence neither do I'.

Tell them you have discovered a remarkable coincidence and hand them the deck of cards and the felt tip pen, which you have specially prepared by allowing it to dry out. Ask them to place the cards behind their back, take out any card, and place an X upon its back.

YOU WILL NEED

A deck of cards

A felt tip pen that you have allowed
  to dry out.

Keeping the deck behind their back, ask them to turn the cards face up, take out any card, and place an X on its face. They must then lose this card in the deck. Once all this has been done, retrieve both the pen and the cards. Place the pen in your inside pocket, thus destroying the evidence and then run through the cards until you come to the only one with an X on its face. Remove it and ask your spectator to find the one with an X on the back.

> ***afTer*THOUGHT** It is a good idea to have a duplicate of the dried out pen to hand that actually works. You can then take out this pen and use it for a follow on effect, thus cunningly demonstrating that the pen wasn't gimmicked!

The spirits write

The final routine in this section and, indeed, the book, is one of my all-time favourites. The principle behind it was very popular with Victorian mediums. They used writing slates, but we will make use of ordinary card to create a spooky effect ideal to present at Hallowe'en, or when a group of you are gathered in a dark room by the light of a lone flickering candle. Enjoy!

YOU WILL NEED

A blank piece of card

A wax candle or bar of soap

A deck of cards.

Prepare the blank card by writing the name of any playing card onto it with the candle or the soap. This writing will, of course be invisible to your audience. Locate that card and put it on the top of the deck. In our example we use the Ace of Spades.

Sit at the table and set the scene. Tell a ghost story to get your audience in the right frame of mind. Ask if they wish to help you contact the spirit world. Hand the cards to a spectator and perform the Turn Over and Cut Deeper Card Force (see page 26). When they have 'freely chosen' the Ace of Spades, ask them to write the name of their card onto a piece of paper and to fold it in half twice, so that you cannot see what is written.

Taking the paper, hold it over the ashtray and set fire to it. Allow it to burn until only a pile of ashes remains. As it burns, wave the blank card over the flames.

Explain that their writing is now in the realm of the spirits, who can use it to answer any questions. Assume your eeriest and most mystical voice and command the spirits to reveal the name of the card in the flames. Dip your fingers into the ashes and rub a quantity of ash over the wax impression. As you do this, the name of the spectator's card will mysteriously appear.

Before you perform the effect

Well you should now have selected a series of effects that you feel you would like to perform before people. You've read and followed the instructions. You've practised until your fingers bleed. You feel confident and ready to amaze your friends, family, work colleagues or even – the public. Surely there can't be anything else you need to do. Well actually there is. The check list.

1. Have you practised the effect until you can do it in your sleep?

2. Have you worked out the stages of your performance when you are most vulnerable to exposure?

3. Have you written down and rehearsed suitable and convincing misdirection to minimise the risk of exposure?

4. Have you worked out what can go wrong with the effect during performance?

5. Do you have a suitable 'out' should the effect go wrong? This should enable you to change the end effect should something go wrong during your performance.

6. Do you know what props or gimmicks you will require for your performance?

7. Have you put them in a place where you can easily reach them? Remember there's nothing more off-putting than being unable to find the appropriate prop or gimmick at the important moment. It results in awkward fumbling.

8. Are you familiar with the area in which your performance will take place? Ensure that your audience will be able to see the magic. Also ensure that they won't be able to see the trickery. Pace around the performance area and see which angles leave you vulnerable to exposing your methods to a member of your audience. Ensure that your audience will be able to hear you; loud music can be a definite problem when trying to control or misdirect your audience's attention.

9. Practise the effect one last time just to be sure.

10. Go out there and amaze them with your magical skills. And remember above all else – enjoy yourself.

*imp*ortant maxims of *magic*

1 Never say beforehand what you are going to do. Forewarned is forearmed. If your audience knows the end result they will have an idea of what to watch out for and will therefore be more difficult to misdirect.

2 Never repeat a trick. You will often find that your audience is so impressed by a particular effect that they ask you to repeat it. To do so is always a bad idea. Firstly, they will be watching very closely the second time around. Secondly, they obviously know, not only the end result, but also the sequence of events that led to it. Only ever repeat a trick if you can achieve the same result with a completely different method.

3 Believe in your magic. One of the most difficult things for a magician to overcome is the fear that the method being employed to achieve the effect is so obvious that the audience will spot it straight away. As you perform each trick, learn to believe in the magic yourself. Act as though you are seeing the effect for the first time and practise being as mystified and astonished as you hope your audience will be.

4 Never perform a trick until you have practised and rehearsed it. It is imperative that you are familiar and comfortable with every part of every effect that you perform. To do this you will need to practise over and over again until you can perform it in your sleep. Take time to analyse the mechanics behind the routines you are demonstrating and see for yourself how your audience will view or perceive the effect.

5 Don't worry if something goes wrong. It happens to every magician. You drop a hidden gimmick; someone opens his or her hand at the wrong moment or sees how you did the trick and tells everyone!! It's not the end of the world. Just learn to laugh it off. Say 'oops' or 'now that surprised me'. You cannot change what's happened so just move on to your next routine.

6 Never reveal your secrets. People will beg you to tell them how you do it. Don't. By exposing your secrets you are belittling the time and effort you have put into your craft. Worse, your audience will not be impressed. Their reaction will be 'oh is that all?'. If someone is really persistent, point them in the direction of your local magic dealer or suggest a good book to get them started, for instance *That's Magic!*

And finally remember
true magic does not happen in the magician's hands it
happens in the spectator's mind.

a MAg*i*cA1 G1oSSARY

Below is a list of words and terms that magicians use. It is a far from definitive list since that would doubtless run into the thousands.

Act: Your act refers to the collected routines you combine into one performance. All magicians have several different acts that they can adapt to suit the occasion and performing circumstances.

Apparatus: This simply refers to the props that you use in your act.

Assistant: Stage Magicians in particular often require an assistant. This is someone with whom you have rehearsed your act and who is an integral part of what you do. Your 'beautiful' [sic] assistant can carry your props onto the stage; select volunteers from the audience; be sawn in half; crushed; fired from a cannon; fired at from a cannon et al.

Back of the Card: The back of the card is the patterned reverse side of the card.

Clean: A favoured term used by magicians meaning that once you have achieved your effect everything can be examined by the audience. Since nothing remains to explain how the magic was done you are clean.

Close-up: This is the most widely performed and effective form of magic today. Your audience is sitting or standing right in front of you and you perform your 'miracles' right under their noses or even in their own hands.

Confederate: This refers to a member of the audience who is actually planted by the magician and who is in on the act. They are also known as a stooge or a plant.

Court Card: These are the royal or picture cards in a deck. The Jacks, Queens and Kings are Court cards.

Cut: To 'cut the deck' is to remove a portion of cards from the top and place them alongside the remainder. To 'complete the cut' you simply place the lower section onto the cut packet of cards.

Ditch: The method by which you secretly dispose of a hidden object.

Effect: What the spectator perceives to have happened in a trick.

Face: This is the value side or front of the card. It's surprising how many people don't realise which side is the face of the card!

Force: To make a member of the audience do exactly as you wish them to do without them realising you've done it! This can involve making them choose a particular card, object, word and so on and so forth.

Glimpse: To secretly look at and note a card's or object's identity.

Gimmick: A hidden device that has been specially manufactured to help you achieve a particular effect. The audience should never see a gimmick nor ever be aware of its existence. It is also known as a gaff.

Indices: The numbers, letters or pips in the corners on the faces of playing cards that denote the suit and value.

Kicker: An extra, often surprise, ending to an effect.

Misdirection: The technique of diverting a spectator's attention away from how or where the trickery is happening. It is the most powerful tool in a magician's arsenal and can be achieved by words or actions.

Move: The secret action by which the final effect is achieved.

Out: Mostly, this is the method by which a magician saves face when things go wrong. When rehearsing an effect it is always good to become familiar with what can go wrong and establish an out to disguise the mistake from your audience.

Pack: A deck of playing cards.

Packet: A small number of cards held together as in when a packet is 'cut' from a deck.

Pasteboard: A widely used magicians' term that simply refers to the playing cards.

Patter: The words used by the performer throughout the performance of an effect.

Presentation: The actual performance of an effect.

Props: The items or materials that you use in the presentation of your act.

Self-Working Trick: An effect that can be achieved without sleight of hand.

Sleight: The secret move by which a magical effect is achieved.

Sleeve: The place that an audience automatically presumes was used to achieve the effect.

Sucker Effect: An effect whereby the audience believes they know how you did the trick or that you have made a mistake, only to have you turn the tables on them.

Vanish: When an object is made to disappear.

Volunteer: A member of the audience who the magician asks to assist him or her with a particular effect or trick.

FURther Reading

Annemann, Theodore. **Practical Mental Magic.** Reprint 1983. *Dover Publications. New York.*

Bobo, J.B. **Modern Coin Magic.** Reprint 1982. *Dover Publications. New York.*

Brandon, Ruth. **The Life and Many Deaths of Harry Houdini.** 1994. *Mandarin Paperbacks. London.*

Buckley, Arthur. **Gems of Mental Magic.** 1947. *Gamblers Book Club. Las Vegas.*

Burger, Eugene. **Spirit Theatre.** 1986. *Kaufman and Greenberg. MD.*

Burger, Eugene. **The Experience of Magic.** 1986. *Kaufman and Greenberg. MD.*

Cannell, J.C. **The Secrets of Houdini.** Reprint 1973. *Dover Publications. New York.*

Christopher, Milbourne. **The Illustrated History of Magic.** 1973. *Robert Hale. London.*

Corinda, Tony. **13 Steps To Mentalism.** Reprint 1996. *D. Robbins and Co. New York.*

Fulves, Karl. **Self-Working Card Tricks.** 1976. *Dover Publications. New York.*

Fulves, Karl. **Self-Working Rope Magic.** 1990. *Dover Publications. New York.*

Fulves, Karl. **Self-Working Paper Magic.** 1985. *Dover Publications. New York.*

Fulves, Karl. **Self-Working Mental Magic.** 1979. *Dover Publications. New York.*

Fulves, Karl. **Self-Working Table Magic.** 1981. *Dover Publications. New York.*

Gardner, Martin. **Mathematics, Magic and Mystery.** 1956. *Dover Publications. New York.*

Hugard, Jean. **Encyclopaedia of Card Tricks.** Reprint 1974. *Dover Publications. New York.*

Jillette, Penn and Teller. **The Unpleasant Book of Penn and Teller or How To Play With Your Food.**

  1994. *Pavilion Books. London.*

Sachs, Edwin. **Sleight of Hand.** Reprint 1980. *Dover Publications. New York.*

Scott, Reginald. **The Discoverie of Witchcraft.** Reprint 1972. Dover Books. New York.

Tarbell, Dr Harlan. **Tarbell Course In Magic.** (6 Volumes). Reprint 1993. *D. Robbins and Co. New York.*

Walker, Charles. **The Encyclopaedia of Secret Knowledge.** 1995. *Rider. London.*

Walton, Roy. **The Complete Walton.** 1981. *Lewis Davenport. London.*

Wilson, Colin. **Mysteries.** 1979. *Granada Publishing. London.*

Wilson, Colin. **The Occult.** 1979. *Granada Publishing. London.*

Wilson, Mark. **Mark Wilson's Course In Magic.** 1988. *Blitz Editions. Leicester.*

where next?

You now have a repertoire of simple magic effects that will impress and astound your family, friends and colleagues. You may choose to leave it at that. However, if this book has whetted your appetite and you wish to pursue your hobby further, here are the names and addresses of several magic dealers, clubs, societies and magazines. Don't be shy about approaching them. You'll find the magical fraternity friendly and welcoming.

MAGIC DEALERS

Davenports
7 Charing Cross Underground Shopping
Arcade
The Strand
London
WC2N 4HZ
(020) 7836-0408

International Magic
89 Clerkenwell Road
London
EC1R 5BX
(020) 7405-7324
www.internationalmagic.com

The Kaymar Magic Co.
189a St Mary's Lane
Upminster
Essex
RM14 3BU
01708 640557

MAGIC CLUBS AND SOCIETIES

The Magic Circle
The Centre For the Magic Arts
12 Stephenson Way
London
NW1 2HD

**The International Brotherhood
of Magicians**
British Ring
Kings Garn
Fritham Court
Fritham
nr. Lyndhurst
Hants
SO43 7HH

MAGIC MAGAZINES

Abracadabra
Published weekly
EDITOR: Donald Bevan
Goodliffe Publications
150 New Road
Bromsgrove
Worcestershire
B60 2LG
(01527) 872246

Genii
Published Monthly
EDITOR: Erika Larsen.
P.O. Box 36038
Los Angeles
CA 90036
USA
001 323 935-2848
The Genii @aol.com

Magic
Published monthly
EDITOR: Stan Allen
7380 S. Eastern Avenue,
Suite 124–179
Las Vegas
NV 89123
USA
001 702 798-4893
www.magicmagazine.com

INdex

The page references to magic routines are printed in bold text. References to published materials are in italics.

acknowledgements

Many people helped with the preparation and research for this book and I thank you all. I must single out Ron Macmillan, whose advice and delightful manner sparked my initial interest in magic; Jo Hemmings for her support and encouragement throughout the project; Martin Macmillan for his useful opinions and advice; Sean East for his observations and objective criticism and Peter Lane at the Magic Circle Library, whose knowledge of magic is unsurpassed. On a personal level I'd like to thank my wife Joanne for her support and for being ever willing to 'pick a card' at the most inopportune moments; my sister Geraldine Hennigan for patiently listening and advising on the text, and finally William Michael Jones, whose sudden arrival as I began the book provided the most magical moment of the whole project!!

The Bicycle Playing Cards used in the photographs are used with the kind permission of The US Playing Card Co., Cincinnnati, Ohio 45212 USA.